Murdo Macdonald, born in 1955, trained as a painter before studying philosophy, fine art and psychology at Edinburgh University. After several years as art-critic for *The Scotsman* he held various academic posts in Glasgow and Edinburgh and in 1997 became the first Professor of History of Scottish Art at the University of Dundee.

World of Art

This famous series provides the widest available range of illustrated books on art in all its aspects. If you would like to receive a complete list of titles in print please write to:

THAMES & HUDSON
181A High Holborn
London WC1V 7QX

In the United States please write to:

THAMES & HUDSON INC.
500 Fifth Avenue
New York, New York 10110

Printed in Singapore

William McTaggart *The Storm*, 1890.

Murdo Macdonald

Scottish Art

183 illustrations, 55 in colour

THAMES & HUDSON

First published in the United Kingdom in 2000 by Thames & Hudson
Ltd, 181A High Holborn, London WC1V 7QX

British Library Cataloguing-in-Publication Data
A catalogue record for this book is available from the British Library

ISBN 0-500-20333-4

Designed by Liz Rudderham

Printed and bound in Singapore by C S Graphics

Contents

Preface

In this book I have traced the art of Scotland from its prehistoric beginnings to the time of writing. The frustration attendant on compressing an account of this extended period into so few words and images, has been lessened by the ever present awareness of shared creative purposes among artists widely separated in time. I hope the book will help the reader to appreciate the intellectual and stylistic textures of Scottish art throughout the centuries, and in doing so, to better understand the cultural condition of Scotland at the beginning of the twenty-first century. My primary debt has been to the work of two people, the philosopher George Davie and the art historian Duncan Macmillan. The former revitalised the study of the history of ideas in Scotland, the latter situated Scottish art firmly within that wider context. Both took the trouble to comment on my text at an early stage. Many other debts will be clear from the bibliography but direct thanks must go to Helen Smailes of the National Galleries of Scotland, Louis Rosenburg of Edinburgh College of Art, Richard Gunn of the University of Edinburgh, and Elspeth King of the Smith Art Gallery and Museum, Stirling, for provision of information at short notice. I must also thank Lorna Waite for comments on the text and unstinting help during the period of writing. A more general debt is to two former editors of *Edinburgh Review*, Peter Kravitz and Robert Alan Jamieson, and to the late Arts Editor of *The Scotsman*, Allen Wright. In the early development of material which became essential to this work the support of former colleagues at the Centre for Continuing Education of the University of Edinburgh, in particular Tom Schuller, was appreciated and thanks must go also to fellow members of the Art and Ideas in Scotland course team, Elizabeth Cumming, Bill Hare, Duncan Macmillan and Andrew Patrizio. Present colleagues in both the Department of History and the School of Fine Art at the University of Dundee have been equally helpful, and the sponsorship, by the Robert Fleming Trust and the Save and Prosper Educational Trust, of my role as Professor of History of Scottish Art at that university, has been invaluable. Finally, warm acknowledgment must go to my editors at Thames & Hudson for intelligent and considerate help throughout.

Murdo Macdonald, University of Dundee, August 1999.

Chapter 1: Prehistory and Early History

Most Scottish art in existence today was made after the Reformation. The period from Neolithic times to the Reformation is therefore presented in this chapter and the one that follows as a preamble. Works from the early period, for example the standing stones of Calanais, the Book of Kells and the stone carvings of the Picts, have nevertheless a high degree of interest both historical and aesthetic and their direct influence is felt in much later work up to the present day.

The First Art

There were people living in Scotland at least nine thousand years ago, establishing communities as the country became habitable in the wake of the last Ice Age but they left little trace until farming became established over six thousand years ago. With agriculture came a more settled lifestyle enabling the establishment of fixed living sites and buildings of wood or stone. Traces of early settlements still survive, for example the interlinked houses at Skara Brae in Orkney which date from between about 3500 BC and 2500 BC. Among the finds at Skara Brae were small objects of carved stone which make an immediate aesthetic impact. They are part of a wider culture of visual and tactile expression throughout Scotland, which includes standing stones, cup and ring marks, maceheads and carved stone balls. These objects all have a quality that brings them into the category of art: they have an unambiguous beauty and their function is psychological, not practical. This is true even in the case of maceheads which, while they derive ultimately from designs for utilitarian objects or weapons, have few traces of wear and it is clear that they were made for symbolic rather than physical use.

Because of the Ice Age, the art of Scotland has no Palaeolithic period, but the Neolithic art such as the standing stones throughout Scotland, in particular the groups sited in and around Calanais in Lewis (*c.* 3000 BC), and the Stenness/Brodgar complex in Orkney, makes a remarkable impact. Martin Martin in 1695 described the Calanais stones as a 'heathen temple'. Over a century later Sir Walter Scott referred to the stones of Stenness as a 'stupendous monument of antiquity... calculated to impress on the feelings of those who behold it'. In 1995 the art historian Duncan Macmillan

1. Standing stones, Calanais, Isle of Lewis, c. 3000 BC. The visual thinking of the early inhabitants of Scotland as expressed by stone circles is of enduring fascination. They relate equally to the landscape and to the skies; aesthetic presence is united with astronomical relevance.

2. Decorated stone, Pierowall, Orkney, *c.* 3000 BC. Most probably a lintel from a chambered cairn, this carving comes from Pierowall on the island of Westray. It seems to have been made by the same seafaring and farming culture responsible for the carvings at Newgrange in Ireland.

3. (opposite) The Towie Ball, *c.* 2500 BC. Rarely found outside Scotland, these beautifully carved objects of stone were probably intended to be held in the hand. They may have been used as symbols of authority within prehistoric communities.

wrote of Calanais that 'these stones were surely the object of pilgrimage'. But getting further than this obvious spiritual and ceremonial function of standing stones is difficult. The fact that they relate with a precise geometry to the features of the land on the one hand and to sun, moon and stars on the other is not in doubt. Whatever their function, these stones leave us in awe of but also in touch with the imagination of the people who created them in the third millennium BC.

On a smaller scale maceheads and carved stone balls are also works of sculptural presence. Maceheads have been discovered at burial sites and this suggests that they have a personal significance. Carved stone balls, however, are not found typically at burial sites and this strengthens the frequently made suggestion that they were symbols of power with a social-ceremonial use, passed from one holder to another, rather than buried along with one person. Perhaps, in the language of these people, the phrase 'holding power' meant literally that. Furthermore, each carved stone ball is markedly different from every other and this distinctiveness again suggests the holding of symbolic power within different groups. About four hundred examples have been found, for the most part between the River Tay and the Moray Firth in the fertile area bounding the southern and eastern edges of the Grampian Mountains. Only four examples of this type of work have been found outside Scotland: two in England, one in Norway, one in Ireland. This uniqueness does not, however, extend to the decorative elements; for example the Towie Ball (*c.* 2500 BC) in its

3

complex spiral design brings to mind the great Neolithic carvings of Newgrange in Ireland and Pierowall in Orkney, despite the difference in scale. Three millennia later this same eastern area of Scotland became the heartland for the making of Pictish symbol stones and understandably enough some archaeologists at first supposed the carved stone balls to be Pictish work.

2

The carving of these stone balls makes one look at them more as sculpture than as archaeological artefacts. The same can be said for the Airdens Macehead from Sutherland (*c.* 3000 BC), which is finished with a pattern of interlocking diamond-shaped facets which produce a surface of subtle beauty. But, unlike the Towie Ball, this macehead finds its echo throughout Neolithic Europe, closely sharing both its form and decoration with works from Merionethshire, Meath and Staffordshire, and all these works share characteristics with contemporary maceheads from the continental mainland. Such cultural connections within Europe at this time can be seen also in the rock art of Argyll. At Achnabreck in 4 the Kilmartin valley a slope of grasses and moss gives way to several hundred cup and ring marks carved in the rock of the hillside. Related sites proliferate in an area of a few square miles. Suggested dates for these cup and ring markings start from around 3500 BC, but they probably continued to be made over the long period which links the Neolithic people who first created stone circles with the Bronze Age people who followed them. Like megaliths and maceheads, cup and ring marks occur throughout Scotland and further afield. They can be found in Perthshire, they

4. Cup and ring marked rock at Achnabreck, *c.* 3500 to 2000 BC. Such markings are usually ascribed to the Bronze Age but earlier dates have also been suggested. They occur throughout Scotland. In the Kilmartin valley around Achnabreck stone carvers created what has been described as a ritual landscape. It is an example of art and land in harmony.

5. (opposite) Battle-axes, *c.* 2000 to 1500 BC. These elegant weapons, found in East Lothian, Aberdeenshire and Lanarkshire, show little sign of wear. Like carved stone balls, it is likely that they were symbols of authority rather than items of use.

can be found near Dundee, they can also be found in Ireland, Northern Spain and Portugal. Various meanings have been suggested for them, ranging from representations of the sun or stars to symbols of the fire so crucial to the process of making bronze. Equally their cyclical quality leads one to speculate that they have some link with the progression of years, months or days. All these notions are plausible enough but open to debate. By contrast, what is very obvious is their siting. The Kilmartin valley has been described as a ritual landscape. Like standing stones, cup and ring marks relate to the wider landscape in a way that makes an immediate impression, complementing the landscape just as the landscape complements them. They are works of what one might call today environmental art. Something here communicates directly and one feels that one is in the same domain of experience as a person from prehistory. But while the communication may be direct, it is fragmentary and incomplete. Whatever I may have in common with a Neolithic or Bronze Age person there is no point in pretending that our societies are similar. Today a decorated bowl of fired clay is commonplace, but in 2000 BC it was an object of high prestige. Something of this reverence for the process of making and using

ceramic vessels of containment has survived in China, Korea and Japan but it has for the most part been lost in the West. At that time Scotland was part of a European culture in which the decorated ceramic beaker was among the most prized of items. Contemporary with these are battle-axes, which differ from the earlier maceheads in their materials and design, yet like those earlier works they have an extraordinary formal elegance.

The Early Celts

Significant for the art of succeeding centuries in Scotland are objects of personal adornment such as a gold lunula or neck plate found at Auchentaggart in Dumfriesshire which dates from about 2000 BC. It follows an Irish pattern which, it seems likely, imitates the form of amber beaded necklaces strung in a crescent shape found as far apart as Mycenae and England. In Scotland there have been a number of finds of similar necklaces made of jet rather than amber, for example from Poltalloch and Melfort in Argyll and from Aberlemno in Angus. Further interest can be found in weaponry. More finely proportioned blades have never been produced than those of bronze leaf swords made in Scotland between 900 BC and 600 BC. Contemporary ceremonial shields of sheet bronze found at Yetholm in the Borders and Auchmaleddie in

Aberdeenshire are 'impressive and finely made' (in the words of T. G. E. Powell). In the third and second centuries BC (the exact dating here is open to debate), a new and distinctive type of design is found in Scotland. It is linked in style both to earlier work in mainland Europe and to work of the historic period in Britain and Ireland. Major examples are a pony-cap and two decorated horn-shaped pieces of metal found at Torrs in Kirkcudbrightshire. When they were found in the nineteenth century all three pieces were assumed to be part of a horned parade mask for a horse and combined in this way they were presented to Sir Walter Scott. This precise combination of the parts is probably wrong, but association with a horse, a pony or a person in the ceremonial role of a horse is accepted. There is an echo here of the poetry of the Rig-Veda at the other extremity of Indo-European civilization: 'His mane is golden; his feet are bronze. He is swift as thought.'

In the Torrs Pony-cap one finds a link to the Celtic La Tène culture centred on Switzerland and southern Germany, the artistic achievements of which resonate across western Europe from about 500 BC until the expansion of the Roman Empire. The Turoe Stone from Ireland is a contemporary and stylistically comparable work. Such work prefigures the contained, cyclical, linear patterns developed in their highest form by the monks of the Celtic Church a thousand years later in the manuscripts now known as the Books of Durrow, Lindisfarne and Kells, and in the high crosses of Iona. The presence of this La Tène style in Scotland raises the question

6

of whether this art was produced by an immigrant community or by a long established local population with European links. There is no clear answer. Archaeological evidence points to Celtic immigration from both southern Britain and Ireland in the first millennium BC. However, Colin Renfrew has argued that the Indo-European language or languages from which the Celtic languages developed spread throughout Europe not primarily as a result of invasion or mass migration but along with the development of agriculture. This would imply that precursors of modern Celtic languages were spoken in Scotland as early as 4500 BC. The argument is helpful. It moves away from the notion that culture can only be transmitted by large scale migration or invasion. Instead Renfrew offers the social-psychological notion that a skill such as agriculture and a language group such as Celtic, go hand in hand. On this view in terms of art one would expect the early inhabitants of Scotland to be receptive to stylistic influences from related cultures even in the absence of significant migration.

The Influence of Rome

In Scotland, the Roman period is characterized by military incursion rather than settlement. There are many traces of Rome but they are for the most part structures with a direct military administrative purpose. Such are the Antonine Wall connecting the Firth of Forth to the Clyde, the great forts at Ardoch on the edge of the Highlands and Trimontium in the Borders, or roads such as Dere Street, the route north from Trimontium to the Forth. In the year 83 it might have seemed that Scotland would follow England and become a Roman province. According to Tacitus that was the date of the battle of Mons Graupius (on an unidentified site between Aberdeen and Dundee), in which Agricola vanquished the Celtic tribes led by Calgacus, killing ten thousand men for the cost of a mere 360 Romans. The historian Michael Lynch has pointed out that this account 'bears the unmistakable ring of the excesses of military memoirs' and perhaps because he was Agricola's son-in-law, accuracy may not have been uppermost in Tacitus's mind. From as early as the year 88 most Roman troops had been withdrawn from Scotland. This may have been as much in response to a need to reinforce the armies on the Danube as because of local resistance. Nevertheless, as Lynch puts it, 'successive Roman attempts to cope with the difficulties of Caledonia's geography are instructive' for from that time onwards the Roman occupation of even southern Scotland was intermittent. One of the most impressive works of Celtic art surviving from this period is

the great boar's head fragment of a carnyx, or war trumpet, from
Deskford in Banffshire (first century). Similar instruments can be
seen on the Gundestrup Cauldron found in Denmark and made
several hundred years earlier. From the same general area and
period as the Deskford Carnyx are massive bronze armlets of
impressive workmanship, sometimes made in a spiral with snake's
head terminals.

In the year 122 Hadrian's wall was begun between Tyne and
Solway as a containment measure, and the same strategy was
applied in Scotland itself with the building of the Antonine Wall
between Forth and Clyde in 147. The fluidity of the situation is
shown by the fact that within fifteen years this new wall had been
abandoned, reoccupied and abandoned again. Finally Scotland
was again occupied as far as the Tay by Septimius Severus in 209,
but, conforming to the established pattern, his new fort at Carpow
on the southern bank of the Firth of Tay was abandoned little
more than two years later. From this time until Hadrian's Wall
was over-run in about the year 400 Roman intervention in
Scotland was limited but not unimportant. In the three hundred
years that Scotland was in direct contact with the Roman Empire
many people living in southern Scotland would have been fluent in
both the local languages and Latin. Later, this clearly facilitated
the development of the Celtic churches of Ninian, Patrick and
Columba. Of great importance also is the fact that the Romans
recorded the peoples and landmass of Scotland in a way that is still
recognizable. It is Tacitus in the first century who calls the area
north of the Forth 'Caledonia'. Another Roman, writing in 297,
first refers to the Picti and the Scoti, nicknames for groupings of
Celtic tribes which have become the familiar basis of Scottish identity today. Similarly important are the occasional examples of
Roman or Roman-influenced art found in Scotland. These are still
being found; for example in 1997 an impressive sculpture of a
lioness devouring her human prey was discovered in the mud of

7. (opposite) Carnyx, 1st century. Found at Deskford in Banffshire, this stylized boar's head functioned as the terminal of a war trumpet. Similar instruments may have been used by the Caledonian Picts in their struggle against the Romans. A war trumpet based on this find and on other evidence has been reconstructed and played.

8. (below) Lioness eating her prey, 2nd or 3rd century. A Roman sculpture found in 1997 in the mud where the river Almond flows into the Firth of Forth at Cramond, on the outskirts of Edinburgh. Cramond was the site of a Roman base supporting the occupation of southern Scotland.

9. (right) Brigantia, early 3rd century. An early combination of classical and Celtic influences, discovered at Birrens in Dumfriesshire. Such a Minerva-like goddess would have been acceptable to both Roman and local sensibilities.

the River Almond, close to the Roman base at Cramond in what is now a western suburb of Edinburgh. An early example in art of the interaction between Celticism and classicism (later reflected in so much post-Reformation Scottish art) can be seen in a relief carving of the goddess Brigantia discovered at Birrens in Dumfriesshire in 1831. This is a Romanization of the goddess of the Brigantes tribe whose territory included what is now Cumbria and south-west Scotland. It combines the attributes of this Celtic goddess (who lives on still in the form of St Bride) with those of the Roman Minerva.

9

Chapter 2:   The Development of Christian Art

Picts and Gaels

When a Roman commentator referred to the Picti and the Scoti, what he was referring to were groups of Celtic tribes united in opposition to Rome. At that time the Picts, together with the Britons, inhabited what was later called Scotland. The Scots or Dal Riata were Irish Gaels rather than Scots in the modern sense although there is archaeological evidence pointing to the cultural continuity of Argyll and the north of Ireland, not only during this period but in the preceding millennia. Indeed, what Christopher Harvie has called the 'inland sea' which extends from the Firth of Clyde to Belfast Lough served in the past more as a channel of communication between mountainous areas than as a territorial boundary. Thus although the Scots became established in Scotland from the fifth century, they were culturally, linguistically, and politically part of a wider Irish grouping until the time of the Viking raids of the ninth and tenth centuries. This linkage can be seen clearly today in the continuum of dialects of Gaelic, which extends from the Highland and Islands of Scotland to the south west of Ireland. Any reference to the Scots before the Viking raids implies this strong Irish connection. Occasionally, to get over this terminological problem, I will refer to Gaels. The political identity of these Scots was clarified around the year 500 with the formal establishment by Fergus Mor mac Erc of a kingdom in Argyll, usually referred to as Dalriada. It included most of modern Argyll along with part of the north of Ireland and it had its capital at Dunadd, an impressive crag that rises abruptly from the flood-plain north of Lochgilphead. Dunadd was the capital of the kingdom of the Scots of Dalriada at the time Columba arrived from Ireland in the sixth century and from Dunadd the route is open to Antrim, Derry and Donegal by way of Jura and Islay. At the top of this fortified hill is a place of installation of rulers. A footprint is cut in a flat rock and beside it is a text in Ogham script. Nearby is an incised image of a boar. This may have been the work of a Scot. Equally, it may have been carved by a Pictish sculptor for such carvings of animals are a characteristic of the Pictish art which survives from the sixth century onwards.

10. Cross slab at Glamis, 8th century. This fine Pictish cross slab has symbols carved both on the face, shown here, and on the reverse. In its interlace design it relates to earlier Celtic/Northumbrian graphic work such as the Lindisfarne Gospels.

11. Papil Stone, 7th or 8th century. This example of stone carving from Papil in Shetland indicates how far north the land of the Picts extended. It also shows the close relationship between Pictish carvings and contemporary gospel illumination, for the lion-like animal which occupies the central panel of this stone is very similar to one occurring in the Book of Durrow.

The interaction of the Picts, Scots and their neighbours is key to the development of art in the following centuries. With the influence of men such as the Briton Ninian of Whithorn in the early fifth century, the Gael Columba of Iona in the mid-sixth century, and the Northumbrian Cuthbert of Melrose and Lindisfarne in the seventh century, Christianity became a force of major cultural significance in Scotland. Pictish art illustrates this, for energy is given to it by a combination of non-Christian and Christian elements. This complementarity of imagery is particularly clear in works such as the Glamis Stone (eighth century). One of the faces of this freestanding red sandstone slab shows incised non-Christian symbols including a salmon and a snake, while the other face is devoted to a very fine knotwork cross executed in low relief and accompanied by images including animals both real and mythical, human figures and symbols. Such early Christianity certainly seems to have been capable of absorbing rather than destroying local belief systems. An interesting example of this from Gaelic tradition is the legend that St Bride was taken from Iona to Bethlehem to be the foster mother of Christ. Thus a Celtic goddess was transformed not only into a Christian saint but also into a figure who was seen to foster the new faith. Although many Pictish clerics would have been literate in Latin, so far as is known the Picts had no written language of their own. Knowledge of them is patchy, reliant only on external commentators and on their art. The 'Picti' of central, northern and eastern Scotland were described by one Roman author as 'Caledonians and others', and this is as good a shorthand as any for a complex grouping which – according to Ptolemy of Alexandria in the second century – was composed of at least twelve named tribes. There is some agreement among scholars that the most likely candidate for the language of the Picts is one closely related to that of Britons. This is certainly consistent both with place-name evidence and with Bede's assertion that the southern Picts were converted to Christianity by the British saint Ninian, for Ninian would have spoken a closely related language. In contrast, in the next century the Gaelic-speaking Columba needed an interpreter in his contacts with the northern Picts. In art the Briton-Pict link is suggested as far north as Shetland in the Papil Stone (seventh or eighth century). The sculptor of this work makes use of a variation of the form of cross found on incised cross slabs of the seventh century and earlier at Ninian's Whithorn at the other extremity of Scotland. Papil is close to an isle named after St Ninian, a place that has a wider importance in terms of Pictish art, for in 1958 a hoard of Pictish silverware was

10

11

12. (below left) Symbol stone at Aberlemno, 6th or 7th century. An early work of Pictish sculpture, which re-uses an existing standing stone. Combinations of symbols, such as the serpent, Z-rod and double disc, occur frequently on Pictish stones. Their meaning is not known, although they may relate to family lineage.

13. (below right) Burghead bull, 7th century. An example of the linear control typical of Pictish animal art. A number of similar carvings were found in the same location at Burghead, Morayshire. They are unusual in that they have no other symbols accompanying them, perhaps indicating that Burghead was the site of a bull cult.

discovered there. It had been concealed from Viking raiders in about 800 and the objects show a very high quality of design and execution. Further fine examples of Pictish metalwork can be seen in objects found at Norrie's Law in Fife. However, the Picts are best known for their stone carving and the first recognized phase of this is in the form of symbol stones which are found extensively in the northern and eastern parts of Scotland. Fine examples come from – among many other locations – Aberlemno in Angus (made 12 a century or more before a cross slab in the same location), Newton in Aberdeenshire and Dunrobin in Sutherlandshire. These symbol stones are evident in the sixth century as pagan or secular statements. Along with symbols of obscure meaning such as Z-rods and double discs, they include images of animals carved with a vivid linearity. These usually occur in combinations of two or more symbols, but in the seventh century images of bulls, probably 13 related to a fertility cult, occur on their own at the coastal fort of Burghead on the Moray Firth. Evident in these works is an ability to draw animals with confident appreciation of their muscularity and weight that has rarely been equalled.

14. Reverse of a cross slab at Aberlemno, 8th century. This image is thought to be a record, carved in the following century, of the crucial battle of Nechtansmere in 685 at which the Picts halted the expansion of the Northumbrians. It is the first clear example of secular representational art in Scotland.

Pictish art was one of the driving forces in the development of the wider Celtic art of this period but its origins are a matter of speculation. The earliest work available is already part of a developed tradition and for this reason it has been suggested by Sally Foster that it is worth reconsidering the neglected theory that the Picts were tattooed, as Roman commentators may be taken to suggest from the very description 'Picti'. Being both linear and compact, Pictish symbol and animal designs are certainly suitable for tattooing and their transmission via such an art is consistent with the existence of a developed visual tradition which left no traces until it appeared carved in stone. But whether the Picts were tattooed or had developed their art in another lost medium such as wood or leather or cloth, they began to carve on stone in the sixth century. Why did they do this? The answer may lie with the increasing political presence of Dalriada. One way in which Pictish symbol stones have been dated is by noting their relative absence from Dalriada and inferring from this that they post-date the establishment of Dalriada. But the shift to stone from another less durable medium may not simply post-date the establishment of Dalriada, it may have been caused by it. With the Scots coming in from Ireland there would have been more pressure to define territory-related authority than previously and this would have been exacerbated by pressure from Northumbria in the south. Perhaps symbol stones from the sixth century reflect this. The social anthropologist Anthony Jackson has suggested that these stones were carved in order to clarify lines of kinship, marriage and authority within Pictland. Such clarification of internal organization is certainly consistent with the placing of the stones well within the Pictish heartland of eastern and northern Scotland rather than as markers of its borders. But what exactly was being clarified? Jackson has opened up discussion of this topic by suggesting that the pairing of symbols can be related in a consistent way to a matrilineal structure of Pictish society, but this interesting idea is far from universally accepted.

The earliest Pictish symbol stones have no trace of Christian symbolism. Later stones, such as that at Glamis, are cross slabs carved in relief, in which the central cross is surrounded by Pictish symbols and images, which might be read as Pictish endorsements of the new religion. With time the cross slabs were carved in deeper relief, symbols taking less of a role and the back of the slab becoming a pictorial field. In an early eighth-century cross slab from Aberlemno this field is a battle scene with men on horseback and it seems reasonable to suggest that this represents a shift from family

14

15. Biblical scene from the St Andrews sarcophagus, probably late 8th century. This remarkable relief carving found at St Andrews in Fife shows Pictish art as part of the art of a Christian Europe in which direct Roman models were no longer easily available, but in which the consciousness of Roman art remained strong.

lineages to a single leader with retinue and army. It is likely that the Aberlemno image shows the crucial defeat of the Northumbrians by the Picts at the battle of Nechtansmere in 685. Here the new imagery records a new politics, a united front against the Northumbrians under the single leadership of the Pictish king, Bridei. But this is also a cross slab, indeed one of the finest, and while it may show the defeat of a Northumbrian army on one side it shows a Christian culture shared with Northumbria on the other. Carved interlace links it to the Lindisfarne Gospels, which were made in Northumbria a few years earlier. Eventually Pictish symbols disappear entirely from the cross slabs. But it is important to emphasize the continuity throughout the whole story. One must also note the geographical continuity between the work of Pictish artists and those working not only in Northumbria but also in Dalriada, in particular at Iona. Such links have led to suggestions that the Iona stone carvers were themselves Picts. Whether this is the case or not, what is clear is the continuity of artistic activity between Pictland, Dalriada and Northumbria. A work in which these interrelationships can be studied is the St Andrews Sarcophagus, thought to date from the second half of the eighth century. It is remarkable in Pictish work both for its unique form and in its commitment to reinterpreting figurative models which derive ultimately from Rome.

16. Detail of the Ruthwell Cross, first half of the 8th century. Some of the finest surviving Northumbrian sculpture is to be found on this cross from Dumfriesshire. Carved also, in runic script, are words from the mystical Anglo-Saxon poem *The Dream of the Rood*.

Northumbrians

Northumbria played an important part in the development of art in Scotland. An early eighth-century cross from Ruthwell in Dumfriesshire, for instance, is among the most significant northern-European monuments of the period. It shows a strong Mediterranean influence in its figurative elements. It also incorporates into its design passages in runic script from the beautiful Anglo-Saxon poem *The Dream of the Rood*, a mystical discourse on the cross written most probably in the late seventh century.

Our knowledge of the period comes largely from the Northumbrian monk Bede whose account, written about 731, is both vivid and sympathetic, although understandably incomplete from a Pictish or Dalriadan perspective. The Northumbrians were predominantly Angles, originally from the borderlands of Denmark and Germany, who had established themselves in eastern and northern England and southern Scotland in the wake of the Roman collapse at about the same time that the Scots established themselves in the the west of Scotland. Like the Romans before them they made periodic incursions into southern Scotland and dominated the area south of the Forth for a considerable period. But unlike the Romans, the Angles of Northumbria were settlers rather than imperial soldiers and their culture became closely related to those of the Picts, Britons and Gaels. At the same time there was considerable political and military tension. The Britons of Strathclyde and Lothian, whose successors in cultural terms are the Welsh of today, made a substantial contribution to the development of visual art but they are most remembered for their Bardic distinction. Their poetry gives rare glimpses of the events of the time. The poet Aneirin, born in Lothian, is best known for lines that refer to the catastrophic defeat of the Britons of Gododdin (whose central stronghold was at Din Eidyn, that is to say Edinburgh), by the Angles at Catraeth (Catterick in Yorkshire) in about the year 600. Three years later the Scots of Dalriada were also defeated by the Angles. By 638 Edinburgh had been captured, and that marked the end of the British kingdom of Gododdin in southern Scotland, although the British kingdom of Strathclyde with its capital at Dumbarton remained. It was another half century (685) before the expansionist King Ecgfrith of Northumbria was stopped for good by the Picts north of the Tay at the battle of Nechtansmere near Dunnichen in Angus, an event recorded, as has been mentioned, on the Aberlemno cross slab. The significance of this defeat is shown by the abandonment soon afterwards of the Northumbrian monastery at Abercorn on the southern side of the Forth. But it was another three hundred years before the united Picts and Scots gained full control of Lothian and the Borders by which time the Vikings were threatening the Northumbrians from York in the south.

Books and Crosses

When told in this synoptic way it is hard to imagine anything but continuous fighting between Picts, Scots, Northumbrians and Britons, but in reality the battles were few and far between and intermarriage between ruling houses very common. Also significant is the frequent use by Northumbrian rulers of Iona as a place of education for their children. There was thus a cultural stability combined with a sense of change sufficient not only to make the development of a sophisticated art possible but also to allow it to flourish to an extent that still astonishes. The exact influence of each cultural group on the development of a shared style is a matter of debate but this art could not have reached the heights that it did had it not been for the interaction of these different traditions. Northumbrian stylistic elements became fused with the art of the Picts, the Gaels and the Britons to produce what is now popularly referred to as Celtic art. A key to this fusion was the establishment by Aidan of Iona of a monastery on the Northumbrian island of Lindisfarne in 635. Carl Nordenfalk evoked the aesthetic power of this relationship when he wrote of Lindisfarne and Iona as 'two poles between which an electric arc of unusual luminous intensity sprang to life'. The Synod of Whitby in 664 was called to resolve dispute over such points as the dating of Easter and the shape of tonsures, and it was the Roman view that prevailed. That event has been seen as the end of a Celtic Christianity which had the potential to unite Columban, Pictish, British and Northumbrian strands into a distinct church. But the Celtic and Northumbrian churches both before and after this date preserved a strong cultural autonomy, most memorably expressed in art. Indeed the second half of the seventh century marks the beginning of two golden centuries of Celtic and Celtic-influenced art, centuries which saw the creation of the cross slabs of the Picts, the manuscripts of Durrow, Lindisfarne and Kells, and the high crosses of Iona and Islay. In addition, there were outstanding secular works of Dalriadic metalwork such as the late seventh-century Hunterston Brooch. The surviving examples were made primarily in Scotland, Ireland, Wales, Cornwall and northern England but also further afield in England and in continental Europe. Lloyd and Jennifer Laing have called the period which has this golden age at its heart, a *renaissance* of Celtic art, a reminder that it developed from an earlier pan-European Celtic culture. It is also a reminder that the history of art is in large measure the history of stylistic revival and development, and that this is just as true in the early historic period in Scotland as it is today.

The Book of Durrow (second half of the seventh century), a work justly described by the Laings as a compendium of European ornamental art, unites influences from the Mediterranean, Northern Europe, Anglo-Saxon England, Pictland and Ireland. It was probably made at Iona but possibly in Northumbria. Its imagery is substantially shared with Pictish sculptors, both in the drawing of animals and birds and in the use of scrollwork spirals. The similarity of the lion-like animal on the Papil Stone and the lion in the Book of Durrow has been widely noted and other examples abound. Similarly the pattern that has been called the 'Durrow spiral', which itself seems to link back to La Tène art, finds its mirror in a lead plaque found at the Brough of Birsay. Papil is in Shetland, Birsay in Orkney, so one finds oneself again looking at a remarkable continuum of late seventh-century Celtic and Northumbrian culture, in which the links between Picts, Britons, Northumbrians and Gaels are as important as the differences. It is thus possible to think of a heterogeneous but coherent school of carving and illumination covering all of Scotland from Iona in the west to St Andrews in the east and to Shetland in the north. The balance of probability is that in terms of drawing animals, stylistic leadership came from the Picts. However, the development of that most subsequently characteristic aspect of Celtic art, knotwork, seems to have come from the adoption of Mediterranean models of interlace in Northumbrian art. This first appears in a developed form in the Durham Gospels and is subsequently taken to a high level in the Books of Durrow, Lindisfarne and Kells. It seems likely that this development was given its energy by the shared maritime experience of the Northumbrians, the Gaels and the Picts, for the complex knot is the mark of a seafaring culture. The final element is the development of decorative and symbolic initial letters and that seems to have had its origins in Ireland. Art in the Scotland of this period can thus be seen as dependent on a vibrant cultural mixture stemming from the northern kingdom of the Picts, the Irish links of the Scots of Dalriada and from the continental European roots of the Angles of Northumberland. The significance of the Book of Durrow is matched by the slightly later Book of Lindisfarne, made at Lindisfarne around the year

17

17. Carpet page from the Book of Durrow (Folio 3v), late 7th century. Made at Iona or a related monastery of the Columban church, this design exemplifies the high level of aesthetic understanding that typifies the great Gospel books of this period.

700, and finally by Iona's last great illuminated statement, made a century later as the Viking incursions began, the Book of Kells.

The Iona-Lindisfarne period of the late seventh century is also the period of two great servants of the church, who were probably born within a decade of each other in the first third of the seventh century. One was Adomnàn, born in Ireland, trained at Durrow and subsequently Abbot of Iona. The other was Cuthbert of Melrose and Lindisfarne. These two church leaders symbolize the difference between the cultural and political life of the time. Real annoyance comes through in Bede's record of the military adventures of King Ecgfrith of Northumbria in his harassment of the Irish, whom Bede clearly regards as friends, and Ecgfrith's subsequent disastrous expedition against the Picts, which Bede makes clear was against the advice of Cuthbert. Similarly, Adomnàn is remembered not only for his Life of St Columba but also for Adomnàn's Law which was concerned with the protection of women, children and clergy during warfare. What is clear is that both Cuthbert and Adomnàn saw Christian culture as necessarily distinct from political and military activity. It is in this context that one can understand the growth of a shared Christian art in spite of military disputes. A highly developed expression is found in the creation of the Book of Kells and the high crosses of Iona towards the end of the eighth century. This period must be seen as a time of unity of artistic experiment and spiritual expression. The artists of the Book of Kells pushed symbolic imagery into a new phase of complexity, but this complexity was driven by a Christian commitment to the word incarnate, the word that was with God and was God, to paraphrase the Gospel of John. All these great illuminated books can be seen as explorations of the idea of incarnation. Here through visual art word becomes flesh and flesh becomes word. The image of the word and the image of the flesh are woven into the same space. It is consistent with the creative nature of this exploration that the greatest discourse on the Gospel of John was written a few years after the making of the Book of Kells by John Scotus Erigena, who was born in Ireland in the early ninth century. At the same time that the illuminators of the Book of Kells were working in the scriptorium of Iona Abbey, the sculptors of St John's Cross were pushing to the limits the form of the stone cross. They overstepped those limits. The cross that stands today in the original location of St John's Cross is a pre-stressed concrete replica, for the stone those early sculptors used was not strong enough to withstand the stresses of combined gravity and wind-speed that their design put upon it. Nothing could better characterize the

21

18. (opposite) St Martin's Cross, east face, 8th century. Fourteen feet in height, this stone cross is one of a number that gives an idea of the sculptural activity on Iona which paralleled the production of works such as the Books of Durrow and Kells. Many crosses have been destroyed but enough survive in and around Iona to indicate the quality of design and execution of which these sculptors were capable.

19. (right) Kildalton Cross, north east face, 8th century. A beautiful cross from Islay, on a smaller scale than those in Iona (about eight and a half feet in height). Some forty miles south of Iona, Islay was very much part of the sea route between Ireland and Scotland.

vision of these sculptors than the fact that it is not until our own time that the structural problem they posed has been solved. St Martin's Cross (mid to late eighth century) and St Matthew's Cross (late ninth or early tenth century) do survive more or less as their designers intended, as does the Kildalton Cross in Islay (late eighth century). After these beginnings in Iona the high cross tradition passes to Ireland and that is outside the scope of

18

19

this book. It can, however, be noted that the radical simplification of the figure to be seen on great ninth-century Irish crosses like that of Moone in County Kildare, finds an echo in the style of the contemporary Book of Deer made in the monastery of that name in Aberdeenshire.

The end of this period when Iona was at the centre of what Arnold Toynbee called 'the originality of this far western Christendom' was signalled by the unforeseen attack by Vikings on Lindisfarne in 793, and in the years following no major monastery in Scotland or Ireland escaped. Eventually in 849 Iona had to be given up as the centre of the Columban church. Despite these difficulties, as the later high crosses show, Iona continued to be important, although the saint's relics and other treasures, notably a book which was presumably the Book of Kells, were split between the new foundation of Kells in County Meath and Dunkeld in Perthshire in 849. What may have been one of these treasures, a beautiful reliquary made of silver, copper alloy and bronze, was supposed to have once contained relics of the saint. It was made in the early eighth century and is known as the Brec Bennoch of St Columba or the Monymusk Reliquary. It is an object of intimate scale the power of which is difficult to understand from a photograph. It would have been worn round the neck, as it was over half a millennium later by a cleric in Robert Bruce's victorious army at Bannockburn in 1314. The metalwork is Pictish but its form is reminiscent of the capstones of Irish high crosses of the ninth and tenth centuries.

The Viking raids of the ninth century began a process of splitting apart the Celtic cultures of Ireland and Scotland, but at the same time they created pressure for the political unification of the Picts and Scots, and this took place in the reign of Kenneth mac Alpin. From the 840s the unified kingdom begins to be recognizable as the predecessor of the modern state. Prior to that date there had been a significant coming together of the two kingdoms even to the point of sharing rulers, but it is an indication of how successfully Kenneth mac Alpin stabilized the situation that he founded the first dynasty of Scottish monarchs. Whether this unity of Picts and Scots came about by conquest, coup or co-operation, or a combination of all three is a matter of debate. What is clear is that from this time onwards the Picts disappear from Scottish history as a named group. Their contribution to the development of art in Scotland had, however, been fundamental.

20. Lewis chess piece, 12th century. This king is part of the collection of twelfth-century chess pieces found at Uig, Isle of Lewis. By the time these chess pieces of Norse design were made, the Vikings had settled from Shetland to Dublin and had become a key component in the ethnic make-up of Scotland.

The Lordship of the Isles and the West Highland School of Sculpture
The period of Norse influence in Scotland which began with the Viking raids of the ninth century lasted until the annexation of Orkney and Shetland from Denmark by the Scottish crown in 1472. During this period Scandinavian culture became one further influence in the art of Scotland. Many of the principles of Norse art such as interlace and zoomorphism are related to Anglo-Saxon and Celtic work, and Celtic art combined easily with Norse influences, for example in a rune-inscribed cross from Barra. Other examples include the Norse-influenced adaptations of the form of the early Whithorn slab crosses such as the Monreith Cross from the late tenth century. Viking influence in Scotland is at its clearest in place-names like Wick and Lerwick on the east coast, and the Gaelicization of the same word (meaning bay or creek) in the west into Uig. It was at one such Uig on the Isle of Lewis that the major find of what is unmistakably Scandinavian art in Scotland was made in the nineteenth century. This is the collection of eighty-two articles of Greenland walrus ivory, mainly chess pieces, now known as the Lewis Chess Pieces (twelfth century). The large number of these pieces, and the fact that some are unfinished, at one time suggested the theory that the collection had its origin in a local workshop but it seems more likely that they were made for trade, perhaps in Trondheim. Neil Stratford has pointed out that 'there is considerable evidence that the "Lewis workshop"

20

belonged to the milieu of Scandinavian Romanesque art of the twelfth century'. This is a reminder that the period of Norse expansion and settlement is the time of the first pan-European style for over five hundred years, the Romanesque, and that in that new Europe the Vikings and their Norman cousins were among the major political players. But whatever their place of origin, the Lewis Chess Pieces reflect the wide cultural links of the western seaboard of Scotland during this period. The thrones of the major pieces bring together side panels which have a Celtic quality to the interlace with seatbacks which recall the scrolled foliage decoration of Norwegian stave churches which were being built during same the period.

To see the Lewis Chess Pieces in a Scottish context one must realise that they were carved at the time of the Lordship of the Isles. This power structure based in Islay reflected the combination of Norse and Celtic influences which gave distinctiveness to the Highlands and Islands of Scotland. It was a time of transition to the late medieval world. European monastic orders had been introduced to Scotland under the influence of Malcolm Canmore's queen, the Saxon princess Margaret. The sons of Margaret and Malcolm Canmore, in particular David I (1084–1153), invited into Scotland a number of Anglo-Norman families who helped to further this mainstream monasticism in Scotland. David I was responsible for the foundation of among others the Cistercian abbey at Melrose in 1136 and the Augustinian priory at Jedburgh, which became an abbey in 1154. The monks at Melrose came from Rievaulx near York while those at Jedburgh came from Beauvais in France. This gives some indication of the strength of the Anglo-Norman influence which brought with it developments in Romanesque and in due course Gothic art. Also from the time of David is the foundation of Dryburgh Abbey in 1150 and in the same year David had raised the status of the Benedictine priory founded by his mother Margaret at Dunfermline to that of an abbey. These Anglo-Norman influences led to the final demise of the practices of the Celtic churches in favour of the standardized rules of Roman Catholic monasticism. But they also led to Iona's second phase of Christian existence as the site of a monastery under the rule of St Benedict, and a nunnery under that of St Augustine.

It is difficult to trace any art directly to Iona at the time of the foundation of the monastery and nunnery, but fine examples of Highland metalwork survive from the twelfth century in the form of the Guthrie Bell Shrine and Kilmichael Glassary Bell Shrine. It is, however, clear that conditions for a thriving art had been created

21. The first words of the Gospel of St John, from the Book of Kells (Folio 292r), c. 800. A century or so after the Book of Durrow, this superlative example of the art of the Columban church was made just as the Vikings were begining to raid Scotland, Ireland and Northern England. The Book of Kells is a high point in the Christian art of Europe during this period but it also marks the beginning of the end of the monastic structures put in place by Columba.

by the new Iona foundations, for from the fourteenth to the sixteenth centuries a highly distinctive contribution was made by the stone-carvers of the West Highland school of sculpture. This began in Iona under the patronage of the Lords of the Isles and in due course centres of activity developed in Oronsay and Kintyre, and around Loch Awe and Loch Sween. These works are both an echo of the art of the Columban church and a direct contribution to the wider Romanesque and Gothic art of Europe. Grave slabs and freestanding stone crosses give a tantalizing glimpse of what may have been lost in other media during the Reformation. Most of this work has the simple purpose of glorifying God while marking the lives of rulers and clerics. In doing so works of a striking beauty were created but at the same time insight is given into what was undoubtedly the most important Norse contribution to Scotland, that is to say technology. On these slabs one sees not only Romanesque vine leaf tracery and echoes of earlier Celtic interlace but clinker-built longships and swords of Viking pattern. By this time the longship had become one of the characteristic features of Highland culture. Differing from the Viking design primarily in the addition of a modern rudder in place of steering oar, these Highland galleys or birlinns appear to elegant effect on many grave slabs and are celebrated by the poets of the period. On a number of later slabs the characteristic Highland version of the European two handed sword, the claymore (*claidheamh mor* in Gaelic) which came into use around 1500, can be seen. Good examples of the carving of both birlinn and claymore can be seen on an Oronsay school work, the Grave slab of Murchadus MacDuffie of Colonsay (1539). Also shown on a number of slabs is that symbol of the shared bardic culture of the the Highlands and of Ireland, the clarsach or harp. On a fifteenth-century slab from Iona a clarsach appears which bears a close correspondence to the Queen Mary Harp, a finely decorated instrument made of hornbeam around 1450, and reputed to have been owned by Mary Queen of Scots in the next century. The survival of these beautiful instruments gives insight into the wider context of music and poetry of which the West Highland sculptors were part.

This late medieval West Highland school of sculpture has been described by Kenneth Steer as 'one of the most remarkable and least understood phenomena in the history of the native arts in Scotland' and this is fair comment. It extends from the time of the Battle of Bannockburn (1314) in which the warriors of the Lord of the Isles played a major part, to the time of the Reformation. Most Scottish art of the period has been destroyed, either by the

22. Grave slab of Murchadus MacDuffie of Colonsay, 1539. The vitality of the pre-Reformation culture of the Highlands and islands is indicated by surviving grave slabs such as this one carved in Qronsay. Note the reminder of the technological contribution of the Vikings in the representation of a Highland galley, the direct descendant of the clinker-built longship.

22

religious unrest consequent on the Reformation or by periodic English invasion. When the abbeys of the Borders and elsewhere, however, were laid waste by the troops of a variety of English monarchs, West Highland work escaped. A further protection from England lay in the fact that there were occasional political alliances between the Lords of the Isles and the Kings of England, for the Lords of the Isles frequently saw their interests as diverging from those of the Kings of Scotland. This tension with the Scottish crown in time led to the demise of the Lordship in 1493. But in terms of art, the Lordship and the associated power-base of the Macleods in Skye, Harris and Lewis had created a degree of cultural stability, which fostered the arts well into the sixteenth century. Outstanding examples of such late West Highland school works can be seen in the Grave slab of Prioress Anna MacLean (1543) from Iona and the Tomb of Alastair Crotach Macleod at Rodel in Harris (*c.* 1540s).

23

23. Grave slab of Prioress Anna MacLean, 1543. The West Highland school of sculpture had its origin in Iona, in that island's second Christian phase as the site of a Benedictine monastery and an Augustinian nunnery. Shown here is a late work of the Iona sculptors, dated just prior to the Reformation.

Chapter 3:   Loss and Reconstruction

Reformation and Rough Wooing

On 11 May 1559 John Knox preached his sermon 'Against Idolatry' in the Kirk of St John the Baptist in Perth. In Knox's own words 'the multitude was so enflamed, that neither could the exhortation of the preacher, nor the commandment of the magistrate, stay them from destroying the places of idolatry'. Following the sermon a mob stripped St John's of art which even Knox describes as glorious and within two days the monasteries of the Franciscans, the Benedictines and the Carthusians – the latter 'a building of wondrous cost and greatness' – had been destroyed so that 'the walls only did remain'. This was not the first iconoclasm of the Reformation in Scotland but it symbolizes its disastrous consequences for art. A further wave during the civil and religious wars of the seventeenth century compounded the tragedy. The ruins of the abbeys of the Borders are moving evidence. But it has been noted that these monasteries founded by Queen Margaret, David I and their successors, had been already despoiled by periodic English invasion and that the iconoclasm inspired by the Reformation merely followed on from this. The case of Melrose Abbey is illustrative. In 1385, two centuries after its foundation, it was completely destroyed by Richard II of England. Rebuilt in a manner strongly influenced by French Gothic, it was devastated by the Earl of Hertford in 1544 and again the next year. Similarly, Jedburgh was ransacked by Edward I in 1297, again by the Earl of Surrey in 1523 and yet again by the Earl of Hertford in 1544 and 1545. The destruction wrought on the Borders by the armies of Henry VIII under Hertford has entered folk memory as 'the rough wooing'. The hand being wooed was that of the young Mary Queen of Scots who was in Henry's view the ideal partner for his only son Edward VI, but this prenuptial disagreement left the Borders in ruins. Those foundations that survive – for example the Romanesque churches of Leuchars and Dalmeny and the abbey of Dunfermline, or the Cathedrals of Glasgow and Kirkwall, the latter founded while Orkney was still under Norse control – can still be appreciated as architecture, but barely a trace of the art they once contained remains. Thus what the religious institutions of pre-Reformation

24. The Annunciation, from the Beaton Panels, 1524–37. Adept carving in a northern-European Gothic manner is evident in this oak panel, part of the flourishing pre-Reformation art in Scotland, little of which has survived.

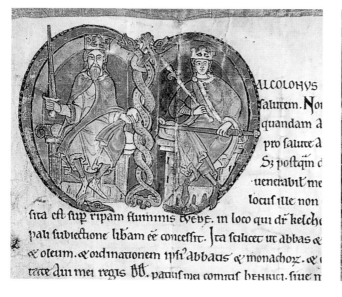

ALCOLOHVS
ſalutem. Noi
quandam a
pro ſalute a
Sȝ poſtqm c
uenerabil me
locuſ ille non
ſita eſt ſup ripam ſiuminis Ꞇueꝺe. in loco qui dꞃ kelchꞓ
pali ſubiecfione libam eē conceſſiꞇ. Jꞇa ſciliceꞇ uꞇ abbas æ
æ oleum. æ oꞃdinationem ipſi abbaꞇis æ monachoꞃ. æ ꞓ
ꞇaꞇe dui mei regis ꞗꞗ. pauuſmei commuſ ᴜᴇʜʀᴜcꞇ. ſiue n

25. (above) Initial from the Charter of Kelso Abbey, 1159 or shortly after. This illuminated initial letter shows David I and Malcolm IV, both key figures in the introduction of Anglo-Norman forms of monasticism into Scotland.

26. (above right) Crucifixion from the Church of Fowlis Easter, second half of the 15th century. The iconoclasm which . was a consequence of the Reformation was so thorough that a complete visual culture has been almost lost. Something of its potential interest is indicated by this work which survived hidden under a coat of paint.

27. (opposite) Matrix of the Seal of the Chapter of Brechin Cathedral, 13th century. Another reminder of pre-Reformation Scottish art. The quality of this seal matrix bears comparison with the high quality of contemporary manuscript illumination in England.

Scotland had to offer in terms of the interacting currents of Celtic and Anglo-Norman art, and in due course Gothic art, is largely a matter of speculation. A few surviving documents, for example an inventory of King's College Aberdeen made in 1542, give some idea of the scale of the loss.

Appreciating the art of the centuries leading up to the Reformation is therefore difficult, and it is easy to assume that with the exception of the West Highland school of sculpture, no coherent body of Scottish art was produced in the thirteenth, fourteenth and fifteenth centuries. But surviving works such as the Celtic Psalter of Irish or Scottish origin, which dates from the tenth or eleventh century, or the Charter of Kelso Abbey (c. 1159), illuminated in a Romanesque style, give a different picture. So also with the thirteenth-century brass seal matrix from Brechin Cathedral which, as George Henderson has pointed out, bears comparison in quality with contemporary English illuminated manuscripts. Again Melrose's defaced statues in fourteenth-century French Gothic style hint at what was once present, while surviving from the fifteenth century is the vigorous sculptural interior of Roslin Chapel (begun 1447). A few significant pre-Reformation paintings survive. Outstanding among these are works from the second half of the fifteenth century in the church of Fowlis Easter near Dundee. These remarkable paintings include an intact representation of the crucifixion, painted over during

25

27

26

the Reformation but never destroyed. Yet what they can tell us is tantalizingly general. It is obvious that Scottish painters of the time played an active part in a northern European tradition, but we don't know whether these paintings were good work by Scottish standards of the time or merely run of the mill. What we do know is that models of the highest quality were available to Scottish artists, for around 1478 the great Flemish artist Hugo van der Goes (*c.* 1440–82) painted *The Trinity Altarpiece* for the Scottish merchant Edward Bonkil and it is a matter of some good fortune that this work survived the Reformation. We also know the quality of work produced in other media. One is left to wonder whether the lost visual art might have matched in transcendent beauty the motets and masses of Robert Carver (1484–1568). Would it have compared in subtlety with the thinking of the theologian John Duns Scotus (*c.* 1265–1308), or that of the philosopher John Mair (*c.* 1470–1550)? (It is a pleasing irony that the latter, in Alexander Broadie's view, almost certainly lectured to both John Calvin and Ignatius Loyola at the University of Paris.) Would it have echoed the nature-imagery that one finds in the poetry of Gavin Douglas (*c.* 1474–1522)? We just don't know.

From the sixteenth century the scattered remnants include fragments of wall paintings in Dunkeld Cathedral and occasional complete works such as a rare textile, the Fetternear Banner (*c.* 1520), and the carved stone sacrament house (1551) in the church at Deskford in Banffshire. This latter work makes an interesting comparison with contemporary West Highland school carving such as the tomb of Alastair Crotach Macleod at Rodel. Further clues about the art of the time come from surviving woodcarvings, in particular the late Gothic Beaton Panels (*c.* 1524–37), which were probably carved by Scottish craftsmen. In contrast, the portrait roof bosses from Stirling Castle (1540), which show a clear understanding of the art of the Renaissance, are almost certainly the work of French craftsmen attached to the court of James V.

It should not, however, be assumed that the loss of religious art led to a loss of all visual expertise. In the area of map-making the reverse was the case, for the years after the Reformation saw the pioneering work of Timothy Pont (*c.* 1560–1630), which led to Scotland in the seventeenth century being one of the best-mapped countries in Europe. The map-maker's father was an influential minister and support for the mapping, carried out between 1583 and 1596, may perhaps have come from the newly reformed church needing to have a better idea of its parishes.

24

SIC BVCHANANVS ORA, SIC VVLTVM TVLIT.
PETE SCRIPTA ET ASTRA, NOOSSE SI MENTEM CVPIS.

ÆTATIS . 76 .
AN°. 1 5 8 1 .

Forty-nine maps based on Pont's drawings were eventually published in Amsterdam in 1654, as part of volume five of Joan Blaeu's *Atlas Novus*.

For the future of Scottish art the most important thing to survive the Reformation was the pattern of cultural and trading links with the Low Countries. These were strongly established

IACOBVS · 6 · D · G · R ·
SCOTORVM
ÆTA · 29 ·
1595 ·

29. Adrian Vanson (attrib.)
James VI, 1595. Following
Bronckhorst, Adrian Vanson
helped to lay the foundation for
Scottish portrait painting, with
works such as this perceptive
image of James VI.

by the fourteenth century, first with Bruges in Flanders and subsequently with the northern provinces that became the Netherlands. The importance of immigration from the Low Countries into the east of Scotland was considerable and it is a further piece of the ethnic jigsaw upon which modern Scotland is founded. It symbolizes a turning point in Scottish culture, away from the older clan-based social organization with its heartland in the Gaelic west to the modernizing influences of commercial Europe focused on the North Sea traders of the east of the country. This cultural link fostered a relationship in painting that had a direct and profound influence on Scottish art right up to the late nineteenth century and was seminal in other fields, such as law and medicine. These Flemish workers had a crucial role in establishing Scotland's weaving industry and one can recall here that both 'Fleming' and 'Bremner' (i.e. Brabanter) are now among the most Scottish of names. After the Reformation Netherlandish portrait painters played a key role in re-establishing Scottish art. Arnold Bronckhorst (*fl.* 1565–84), who has links with the English miniaturist Nicholas Hilliard, came to the court of James VI in 1580. He was followed by Adrian Vanson (*fl.* 1580–1601), and Vanson was probably the painter of a perceptive image of that ambitious and single-minded monarch in 1595. Eight years later James succeeded to the English throne.

28

29

George Jamesone and the Rebirth of Scottish Painting
The Union of the Crowns in 1603 and the consequent move of the court to London resulted in a further loss of patronage for Scottish artists. In consequence the art of seventeenth-century Scotland is sparse. But it is also interesting and some hint of what was to come can be seen in a portrait from 1616 of the inventor of logarithms, *John Napier of Merchiston*, by an anonymous Scottish painter, possibly John Anderson (*fl.* 1600–1649). The Netherlandish input continues in the work of Adam de Colone (*fl.* 1622–28) the son of Adrian Vanson. Most significantly the first Scottish painter in the modern sense emerges. The importance of George Jamesone of Aberdeen (*c.* 1589–1644) lies in the fact that he fully comprehended the lessons of Netherlandish portrait painting. He trained in Edinburgh with John Anderson and was clearly aware of the developments of his age, including the work of Anglo-Netherlandish artists such as Cornelius Johnson (159 *c.* 1662) and Daniel Mytens (*c.* 1590–1642). With works like *Erskine, Countess Marischal* (1626) and his own *Self-* (*c.* 1637–40), against a background of paintings, Jameso

30. **George Jamesone**
Self-portrait, c. 1637–40.
Jamesone was the first Scottish-born painter to make a major contribution after the Reformation. Here he shows himself at the heart of the products of his profession, at one with the variety and international scope of the painter's art.

31. (opposite) *The Muses and ~ues*, 1599. This painted
~ at Crathes Castle reflects
~us late-Renaissance
~. One can sense an
~ culture remaking
~e loss of the
church.

considered the founder of the Scottish school of portraiture which was to find its highest expression in the works of Allan Ramsay and Henry Raeburn in the next century.

Sculpture was relatively insignificant as an independent art in Scotland during this period and it continued to be so until the early nineteenth century. However, there were some notable statues made in architectural contexts, for example the figures of *Justice* and *Mercy* carved in 1637 for Parliament House by Alexander Mylne (d. 1643) and the extraordinary grave sculptures of Greyfriars Kirkyard in Edinburgh. Indeed it is in architecture that experimentation in three dimensions was truly active, notably with respect to new possibilities for plastic expression as the form of the fortified tower house became an aesthetic opportunity rather than a defensive necessity. Fine examples of this are the castles of Crathes, Fyvie, Craigievar and Glamis. Some of these buildings boast remarkable ceiling paintings of humanist inspiration and vigorous design, such as *The Muses and Virtues* at Crathes, painted in 1599. In formal gardens created at the same time are examples

31

KG

Low companions take your leaue to mee · To play on lute. I haue protest · All trouble myding to make·

Quick memorie ano sharp. Imora. Adlemios will take semmms·

My monicordis my well expresse · Promemm the luth tri vou ·

32. John Michael Wright
Sir William Bruce, 1664.
Wright was Jamesone's most distinguished pupil. He was capable of a high degree of sensitivity to the character of his sitters, as here in his portrait of the pioneering Palladian architect Sir William Bruce.

of multifaceted sundials, which, as late-Renaissance conjunctions of art and science, are resonant with the last years of alchemy and the development of Freemasonry.

George Jamesone's death in 1644 coincided with the disruptions of the Cromwellian period both north and south of the Border. Artistic activity during the mid-century was limited. The 1650s saw the emergence of David Scougal (1598–1661) as a painter. He is particularly remembered for his searching portrait of Archibald Campbell, Marquis of Argyll (*c.* 1655), the Presbyterian leader who had crowned Charles at Scone in 1651. (After the restoration of Charles to the English throne the political sands shifted and Campbell was executed on the King's instructions in 1661.) By contrast the Restoration benefited George Jamesone's pupil John Michael Wright (1617–94), so much so that he styled himself 'king's painter'. This talented artist was a native of London but had strong Scottish connections and was probably of Scottish parentage. He was apprenticed to Jamesone in Edinburgh for five years from 1636 and spent much of the 1640s in Rome where in 1648 he became a member of the Academy of St Luke alongside Velasquez and Poussin. Wright was a less fine technician than his contemporary at the court of Charles II, Sir Peter Lely (1618–80), but he was the better perceiver of human character. Rarely has a man been more sensitively portrayed than in Wright's portrait (1664) of *Sir William Bruce* (1630–1710), the architect who extended the Palace of Holyroodhouse for Charles II and set Scottish architecture on a Palladian road. Yet as a portraitist Wright was matched by the miniaturist David Paton (*fl.* 1668–1708). In his portrait of *Lord Mungo Murray* in Highland dress, probably painted in Ireland in the early 1680s, Wright made an early image of a type which has gained strength as an icon of Scottishness ever since. In his portraits of William Bruce on the one hand and Mungo Murray on the other, he created a synopsis of the classical and Celtic currents in Scottish thought which were to be worked out both in combination and in conflict in the next century.

A Grammar of Painting in Place
The continuing importance of the Netherlands can be seen in the appointment by Sir William Bruce of Jacob de Wet (1640–97) to paint decorative schemes at Holyrood. De Wet's significance extends further than this for he also painted still lifes and genre scenes, such as his *Highland Wedding* for Sir John Clerk of Penicuik, in the closing decades of the seventeenth century. This

latter theme reaches its finest expression the work of David Wilkie well over a hundred years later. The seventeenth century is thus the time when a thematic grammar was established from which the discourse of Scottish painting developed. An element that has not been mentioned is landscape. Again it is from artists of the Low Countries that the earliest works come, for example a view of *Falkland Palace and the Howe of Fife* painted for Charles I in the 1630s by Alexander Keirincx of Brussels (1600–1652). Some Scottish artists made more of a contribution abroad than in their own country. Indeed the most talented Scottish exponent of still life at the time, William Gouw Ferguson (1632–c. 1695), is more properly considered as part of Dutch painting, although several of his works made their way back to Scotland. Ferguson is one of a number of Scottish painters who made their careers elsewhere in Europe. James Hamilton, too, began his career in Edinburgh but developed it in Germany and the Low Countries. He died in Brussels in about 1720.

The year 1689 saw the acceptance of the Crown of Scotland by William and Mary and in response to this the first Jacobite rising. This culminated in the death of John Graham of Claverhouse, and the end of Jacobite hopes at the Pyrrhic victory of Killiecrankie. The coming of William was a glorious revolution indeed from the perspective of many Presbyterian Scots, particularly those Covenanters who had suffered brutal persecution during the 'killing time' of the reign of Charles II. However, it was distinctly inglorious from the perspective of clans such as the Macdonalds of Glencoe, who were massacred as Jacobite sympathizers in 1692 as part of a government strategy to use terror as a means of social control in the Highlands. In London these political tensions are reflected in the life of John Michael Wright, who as a Jacobite suffered eclipse after the coming of King William. He died in 1694, out of favour and in relative poverty.

The last figure from the Low Countries to make a major contribution to Scottish art was Brussels-born Sir John de Medina (1659–1710). He was persuaded to move from London to Scotland by the Earl of Leven in 1693 to fill the gap left by the death of David Scougal in 1680, for Scougal's son (or nephew) John was not the painter his father had been. Medina was an outstanding portrait painter in the mould of Sir Godfrey Kneller (1646–1723). He has a unique place in the history of Scotland for he was the last person to be knighted by the independent Scottish Parliament prior to the Union.

34. **Thomas Warrender**
Allegorical Still Life, *c*. 1708.
This intriguing painting dates from
just after the union of the Scottish
and English parliaments. It has
evaded full interpretation but
seems to assert the power of the
word over that of princes, and as
such it restates the tenets of much
Scottish Reformation thinking.

Chapter 4:   Classicism and Celticism

The new century saw parliamentary union with England in 1707. Reflecting on the political complexities of the time, Thomas Warrender (*fl.* 1673–1713) painted an illusionistic image of a letter-board (1708 or after). It is difficult to interpret Warrender's meaning fully, but he seems to be both invoking the Union as a defence of Presbyterianism and reminding those who held power in the Union to honour the letter of the Union and defend Presbyterianism. Either way this image claims the priority of the word over the rule of princes for the image contains a copy of the Solemn League and Covenant and quill pens which point down to an image of a king, either Charles II or James VII and II. The assertion of the limited power of the monarch is a recurrent theme in Scottish history, finding its first expression in the Declaration of Arbroath in 1320. It had been restated during the Reformation by George Buchanan (*c.* 1506–82) and subsequently by Samuel Rutherford (*c.* 1600–1661). One senses in Warrender's emblematic painting an echo of both Buchanan's *De Jure Regni* of 1579 and Rutherford's *Lex Rex* of 1661.

A Landscape made Classical

Warrender made his living as a decorative painter working closely with architects. He may well have been the teacher of James Norie (1684–1757) who likewise worked closely with architects, in particular William Adam (1689–1748). Norie and his sons James (1711–36) and Robert (d. 1766) made classically inspired landscapes for installation as panels conceived of as integral parts of interiors. Initially these works were simply contributory to the great classical architectural project of eighteenth-century Scotland, but as the century progressed the painters emancipated themselves from their role as decorators. The Norie family produced a number of landscapes which are strongly indebted, via engravings, to painters active in Rome in the previous century, in particular Gaspard Dughet (1613–75) and Claude Lorraine

34

35. **James Norie** (with additions by **Jan Griffier II**) *Taymouth Castle (from the South)* 1733 (repainted 1739). Norie is a key figure in the development of the art of landscape painting in Scotland. He and his sons brought to Scottish art the influence of Claude, Poussin and other painters of seventeenth-century Rome.

36. (opposite) **Jacob More** *The Falls of Clyde: Cora Linn*, 1771. Apprenticed to the Norie family, Jacob More took the integration of ideal landscape and Scottish reality to a high point in his response to the Falls of Clyde. He later settled in Rome.

(1600–1682). A more immediate influence was the English theatre scene-painter George Lambert with whom the brothers James and Robert studied in London. In 1733 a topographical view of Taymouth Castle was painted for Lord Glenorchy as a record of William Adam's redesign of the landscape of the property. This work, which has later additions by Jan Griffier to reflect subsequent changes in the grounds, is probably by James Norie senior but possibly by his son of the same name. It begins a dialogue in Scottish painting between Claudian principles and Scottish realities of which a further early example is Robert Norie's *Landscape with Ben Lawers* (1741). A presumed student of Robert Norie was Charles Steuart (*fl.* 1762–90) who produced remarkable Perthshire landscapes for the Duke of Atholl at Blair Castle, such as *The Black Lynn, Fall on the Bran* (1766). The Claudian strand was taken to an extreme by another painter apprenticed to Robert Norie, Jacob More (1740–93), who eventually settled in Rome to devote most of his time to Claude-inspired landscapes. These are such an act of homage that More's own character as a painter is almost lost. That he had such a character is very clear from his series devoted to *The Falls of Clyde* (1771) which he carried out before leaving for Rome. He was influenced in these works by the French artist Claude

Vernet (1714–89), whose *Landscape with a Waterfall* (1746) was hanging at Dalkeith Palace. Another artist who had his roots in the decorative painting tradition must be mentioned. Richard Waitt (*fl.* 1708–1732) produced some of the most remarkable portraits of the early eighteenth century for the Lairds of Grant. Waitt was never formally trained as a portrait painter and his works have a naive quality. But this very quality goes straight to the heart of the subject, as in his painting of *Nic Ciarain, The Hen-wife of Castle Grant* (1726). Also employed by members of the Grant family was John Smibert (1688–1751). Smibert's real importance lies outside Scotland, for in 1728 he took ship with the Irish philosopher and churchman George Berkeley with the intention of helping him to found a college in the Bermudas. The scheme came to nothing but Smibert settled in Boston in 1729 to become one of the founders of American painting.

Artists and Intelligentsia

James Norie senior was a close friend of the poet Allan Ramsay (*c.* 1685–1758), who as well as being Scotland's most eminent literary figure of the time was a strong advocate of the visual arts. Along with Ramsay, in 1729 Norie helped to found the Academy of

38

THE HEN WIFE
Castle GRANT
A. D. 1706

37. (opposite) **William Aikman** *Self-portrait*, possibly *c*. 1712. Aikman introduces a new type of Scottish artist, the member of a cosmopolitan intelligentsia. Here he portrays himself with the painterly confidence of his teacher Sir John de Medina.

38. **Richard Waitt** *Nic Ciarain, The Hen-wife of Castle Grant*, 1726. Waitt's relative isolation as painter to the Grant family, contributed to the independence of his vision. This is one of a series of vivid, almost naive, portraits which comprise an invaluable record of rural roles in eighteenth-century Scotland.

St Luke, Scotland's first art school, in Edinburgh. Named after its great counterpart in Rome, it was more a small training studio for practising artists than an art school in the modern sense. Although it only lasted for three or four years it was the first place of professional training for artists in Scotland through a school system rather than by trade apprenticeship. Those who signed the charter in 1729 were a distinguished group of early-Enlightenment figures which included William Adam. Another was the portrait painter William Aikman (1682–1731), whose first teacher had been Sir John de Medina, to whom he had been introduced by his cousin, Sir John Clerk of Penicuik. Reversing the direction of Medina's travels Aikman, having established his reputation in Edinburgh, continued his career among the new Scottish Parliamentary community in London. These were the years immediately after the Jacobite rising of 1715 had petered out and in London Aikman enjoyed the patronage of the Hanoverian leader, the second Duke of Argyll. Aikman was a confident and engaging painter whose

37

debt to Medina is clear. He was educated at Edinburgh University and studied his art in Edinburgh, in London and in Italy where he undertook an extensive Grand Tour. He thus introduced the notion of the eighteenth-century Scottish artist as a member of a cosmopolitan Scottish intelligentsia. Such perception of the role of the artist, is made clear in a painting by Roderick Chalmers (*fl.* 1709–30) which dates from 1720. It is entitled *The Edinburgh Trades* and although painting is represented as one of these trades, the image of the painter, a portrait of Chalmers himself, is not that of a tradesman but of a gentleman in wig and velvet coat. A witty and assertive statement, it draws attention to the incipient Enlightenment milieu of Edinburgh, which was to bring together the visual, the literary and the philosophical.

Another signatory of the charter of the Edinburgh Academy of St Luke was John Alexander (1686–*c.* 1766). Like Aikman, Alexander studied in London and Italy as well as in Scotland, and his Baroque sketch of *Pluto and Proserpine* (1720) for the ceiling of Gordon Castle – the ceiling itself is long gone – has a particular interest as the only surviving work by a Scottish artist in that style. In Rome he painted many of the expatriate Jacobite community and he was followed in this by his son, Cosmo (1724–72), also a distinguished artist. John Alexander was from Aberdeen and most of his career was spent in that area. He was out with the Jacobites in the rebellion of 1745 which led to him being declared a wanted man in 1746 but a few years later he was again able to paint openly. When he died in 1766 he was engaged in an early example of the painting of an event from Scottish history, the escape of Mary Queen of Scots from Loch Leven Castle. His younger Aberdonian contemporary William Mosman (1700–1771) also studied in Rome. Although both Alexander and Mosman worked predominately in the north-east, both produced images of key figures in early-Enlightenment Edinburgh. Alexander painted *George Drummond* (1752), the Lord Provost whose vision led to the building of Edinburgh's grid-patterned New Town. Drummond is shown with another cherished project, William Adam's newly finished Royal Infirmary, the more appropriate as a subject because John Alexander was himself the son of a doctor. Mosman painted one of Scotland's financial pioneers, *John Campbell of the Bank* (1749). This interesting picture shows a Hanoverian Whig, sufficiently secure in his loyalty to the government to insist on being portrayed in Highland dress at the time of its proscription after the failure of the '45 Rebellion. At the same time he is shown – banknote in hand – in his role at the heart of the development of

Lowland commerce. This period also saw the blossoming of the career of William Adam's son Robert (1728–92), subsequently one of the most influential of all European architects. Robert Adam's thinking was devoted both to the development of classical architectural form and to the idea of the building in a landscape. His place on the edge of the Scottish landscape tradition can be noted, for he produced remarkable wash drawings of imaginary landscapes. He was a friend of the English watercolour artist Paul Sandby (1725–1809), who made a number of influential drawings of the Highlands while employed by the Board of Ordnance in the wake of the '45. Sandby was the main draftsman for the survey of the Highlands carried out by David Watson and William Roy from 1747–55.

With Robert Adam's generation one finds Scottish painters beginning to fully enter the European mainstream. Foremost among these was Allan Ramsay (1713–84), son of the poet of the same name. Ramsay was not only an artist of the highest order, he also played a leading role in the intellectual life of the time. In Edinburgh in 1754 he was a founder, along with his close friend David Hume (1711–76) and Hume's fellow philosopher Adam Smith (1723–90), of the Select Society. The same period saw the writing of his *Dialogue on Taste*. The interaction of artists and philosophers made possible by the Select Society was complemented by continuing efforts to provide schools for the development of professional artistic skills. In Glasgow substance was given to such training by the foundation of the Foulis Academy in 1754, in Edinburgh by the foundation in 1760 of what became known as the Trustees' Academy, the first municipal design school in Scotland and indeed in Britain. The trustees in question were those of the Board for Fisheries, Manufactures and Improvement in Scotland, and they included Lord Provost Drummond himself. The municipal status of the Trustees' Academy underlines the fact that art and design were increasingly considered to be part of civic life, not simply as the province of aristocratic patronage. The first master of the Trustees' Academy was the French artist William Delacour (*fl*. 1740–67), whose most resonant work from this civic perspective is a view of *Edinburgh from the East*, painted in 1759. Allan Ramsay's early training had been at the rudimentary St Luke's Academy which, as has been noted, his father had helped to set up in Edinburgh. He soon took his studies further in London – where Hogarth's directness of approach was no doubt an influence – a in Italy where he studied with the painters Imperiale in Rom Solimena in Naples, returning to establish himself in Lo

1738. Ramsay's great ability as a painter was to interpret the face as a form in space informed by sympathy. Given confidence by his studies in Italy, his starting point is nevertheless the cool light of northern Europe and no artist has better grasped its quality than Ramsay in his portrait of *Anne Bayne*, his first wife (1743) 41 and his own *Self-portrait* from about 1740. He maintained strong

JOHN
-1777

40. **William Mosman** *John Campbell of the Bank*, 1749. Secure in his loyalty to the house of Hanover, Campbell has the confidence to wear tartan despite its proscription after the Jacobite defeat at Culloden in 1746.

contact with Edinburgh and revisited Italy when he could, but like William Aikman he spent much of his career serving the needs of the expatriate Scottish community in London. Of particular significance was the patronage of the Earl of Bute who recommended him to the Prince of Wales, the future George III. Ramsay painted his first portrait of the Prince in 1757 and in due course

41. **Allan Ramsay** *Anne Bayne*, c. 1740. With Ramsay, Scottish painting takes its place alongside the best in Europe. He married Anne Bayne in 1739 and here he evokes her presence with an extraordinary sensitivity to the fall of light.

42. (opposite) **Allan Ramsay** *Hew Dalrymple, Lord Drummore*, 1754. Ramsay's intellectual pursuits are reflected in his role as a founder member, along with David Hume and Adam Smith, of the Select Society in Edinburgh. Another member was Hew Dalrymple, who is shown here both assured and thoughtful.

established himself as a painter of royal portraits. In a number of these works he was assisted by David Martin (1737–97), a notable Scottish artist in his own right. But even at the height of his success as a royal portraitist Ramsay's most notable contribution lay not in his images of robed figures of state but in more direct and intimate work. This personal approach is extended to royalty in his remarkable portrait of *Queen Charlotte with a Fan* (c. 1763), but it is seen with particular clarity in works such as *Hew Dalrymple, Lord Drummore* (1754). In the latter, with confidently weighted balance of tone Ramsay shows the character of one of his friends in the Select Society. A more sensual intimacy is reflected in the shimmer of brushwork that evokes the features of *Mrs Bruce of Arnot* (c. 1765) and *Margaret Lindsay* (early 1760s), the artist's second wife. In those works he brings to mind the contemporary pastels of Maurice-Quentin de La Tour (1704–88) in France. Ramsay's philosophical interests are reflected in his portraits of *David Hume* (1766) and, painted as a gift for Hume,

42

43

44

Jean-Jacques Rousseau (1766). It is appropriate that it is through the works of Allan Ramsay, the scholar-painter, that the world remembers the features of the two philosophers today. Ramsay spent his last years pursuing a long-term interest in the location of Horace's villa near Rome, a project in which he enlisted Jacob More's skills as a topographical artist. In this quest for a place that might give sense to the relationship between poet, society and land one finds an echo of the pastoral and folk interests of Ramsay's father and also of the wider concern with the nature of society which was shared by Enlightenment thinkers in general.

Hamilton's Iliad

Allan Ramsay died at Dover in 1784 while returning from his fourth trip to Italy. His contemporary Gavin Hamilton (1723–98) made his whole career in Rome. Hamilton studied Humanities at Glasgow University under Francis Hutcheson, who was a strong supporter of the arguments advanced by the Earl of Shaftesbury in favour of the superiority of ancient Greek culture. In the mid-1740s Hamilton travelled to Italy to train as a painter and in Rome he studied with Agostino Masucci. Robert Rosenblum has noted the 'priority which British, and particularly Scottish, painting had in the introduction of classic style and iconography in the second half of the eighteenth century' and Hamilton is a key figure here.

43. (opposite) **Allan Ramsay**
Margaret Lindsay, early 1760s.
Ramsay's portrait of his second wife looks forward to Wilkie in the immediacy of the relationship between painter and sitter.
Horace Walpole described Ramsay's painting as 'all delicacy', and in this work it is clear what he meant.

44, 45. **Allan Ramsay**
David Hume and *Jean-Jacques Rousseau*, 1766. The pair of portraits which Ramsay painted for his close friend David Hume – of Hume himself and of Jean-Jacques Rousseau – have become the standard images by which the faces of the philosophers are remembered.

46. **Gavin Hamilton** *Achilles lamenting the death of Patroclus*, 1760–63. Part of a major project of large-scale paintings which illustrate passages of Homer's *Iliad*, in this work Hamilton involved himself in the Enlightenment project of exploring the origins of civilization and the source of the customs and moral values of the present.

Indeed, it is almost as though in the second half of the eighteenth century one of Scotland's art schools was in Rome with Gavin Hamilton as the informal principal. Along with the German painter Anton Raphael Mengs (1728–79), Hamilton pioneered eighteenth-century neo-classical painting from the 1750s onwards, influencing among others the Frenchman Jacques-Louis David (1748–1825). Hamilton's paintings are Enlightenment speculations about the origins of society and political organization. In his *The Death of Lucretia* (1768) he explores the suicide of Lucretia, an event thought of as fundamental to the birth of the Roman Republic and hence to the political and social history of Europe. Similarly, in a major cycle of six very large canvases he illustrates passages from the fundamental text of European literature, the *Iliad* of Homer. 46

The first of these, *Andromache Bewailing the Death of Hector*, was completed in 1761 and shows Hamilton's clear interest in Poussin's *Sacraments*. Although these *Iliad* works were commissioned by different clients, Hamilton early on planned them as engravings (most of which were carried out by Domenico Cunego), thus ensuring that the narrative cycle was widely available in its entirety. These works echo the influence of Hutcheson and Shaftesbury and act as a visual parallel to the influential *Inquiry into the Life, Times and Writings of Homer* published in 1735 by the Aberdeen scholar Thomas Blackwell. Hamilton was also a notable archaeologist and this side of his activities is reflected in his painting of *James Dawkins and Robert Wood Discovering Palmyra* (1758). The wider search for first principles in all fields to which Hamilton contributed can be seen not only in the philosophical and artistic activity of the time but also in pioneering scientific work. This included that of the geologist James Hutton, the chemist Joseph Black, physicians such as William Cullen and engineers such as James Watt and Thomas Telford. Like late-Habsburg Vienna and Weimar Germany, this period of Scottish culture was one of high intellectual and artistic productivity driven by well-educated, innovative thinkers living in a society subject to considerable political stress. One can summarize this by noting that Hume's philosophical works *A Treatise of Human Nature* and *An Enquiry Concerning Human Understanding* were published in 1739 and 1748 respectively, neatly bracketing the Battle of Culloden in 1746.

The Origin of Painting

The exploration of first principles was developed in terms of the foundation of painting itself by two of Hamilton's followers in Rome, Alexander Runciman (1736–85) and David Allan (1744–96). Both painted versions of the legend of the *Origin of Painting*, Runciman in 1773 on his return to Edinburgh and Allan in Rome in 1775. They follow Pliny's story of a young Corinthian woman, daughter of a potter, outlining the shadow of her lover on a wall before he departs to war. Runciman's focus was on the primary motivation of art, namely feeling, for Cupid guides the hand that draws. Allan reflected also on the optical process, emphasizing the single point source of lamp-light which gives the shadow its size and makes it sharp enough to trace. Thus the concerns of Runciman and Allan were not simply with the retelling of a quaint legend about primitive painting practices. That contrasts with earlier versions of related subjects which stretch back at least as far as Murillo. Rather, both artists were engaged in psychological

50

commentaries, typical of the Enlightenment, about what might constitute the minimum conditions of representation. They addressed issues both social and perceptual within a framework which, following Dugald Stewart, one can call conjectural history. In these works they asserted that art is founded first of all on human relationships and secondly on the act of representation and abstraction. It is in this context that one must understand subsequent careers. While in Italy, Allan had shown a strong interest in depicting scenes from everyday life and on his return to Scotland he developed as a genre artist, painting subjects such as *Highland Wedding, Blair Atholl* (1780), and making illustrations for the poet Allan Ramsay's *Gentle Shepherd*. This should not be seen as a fall from grace from the supposed higher reaches of history painting to the supposed lesser art of genre. The two were, for Allan, part of

47

48. (below) **James Tassie** *Robert Adam*, 1792. David Allan's friend James Tassie mastered a technique of fusing glass paste to create classically inspired portrait medallions of figures of the Scottish Enlightenment. This example shows the architect Robert Adam.

49. (below right) **John Kay** *Self-portrait*, 1786. Like the medallions of Tassie, John Kay's etched portraits of Edinburgh figures are an invaluable reflection of the time. His own self-portrait is a witty commentary on the domestic classicism of Enlightenment Edinburgh.

the same project of investigating the human condition. Allan turned to the Highlands and to the Lowland folk tradition for examples of societies which might still be in touch with the customs of an earlier, more socially cohesive age. In a similar search for alternatives to the increasingly urban present, Alexander Runciman turned to Celtic mythology as reinterpreted by James Macpherson (1736–96) in *Ossian*, a prose-poem cycle first published in the 1760s and based in part on Gaelic oral tradition. Hamilton's *Iliad* paintings find an intriguing counterpoint in this aspect of Runciman's work. Thus Allan turning to the folk tradition as mediated by Ramsay and Runciman's development of Celticism as mediated by Macpherson must be seen as related projects.

One of Allan's close friends was James Tassie (1735–99), who created profile-portrait medallions in fused-glass paste inspired by classical cameos and intaglios. Both artists were educated at the Fowlis Academy in Glasgow. They became in due course lifelong collaborators, Allan often illustrating Tassie's catalogues. Tassie's career in Glasgow, Dublin (where he learned his glass paste technique) and London shows that the strength of the classical

48

JOHN KAY
Drawn & Engraved by Himself 1786.

50. **David Allan** *The Origin of Painting*, 1775. Allan was Gavin Hamilton's pupil in Rome. Here, rather than exploring the origins of society, he makes his focus the perceptual and social origins of painting itself as recounted by Pliny, in one of the earliest eighteenth-century explorations of this theme.

inspiration in Scotland did not always depend on visiting Rome. He returned to Edinburgh and Glasgow frequently and the list of his sitters reads like a *Who's Who* of the Scottish Enlightenment. The self-taught John Kay (1742–1826) took this project of illus- 49 trating the intelligentsia further. In the 1780s Kay made inspired caricatures of the cultural community of Edinburgh which owe much both to Allan and to Tassie.

Runciman's Ossian

Mention must also be made of Alexander Runciman's younger brother John (1744–68), who died in Rome at the age of twenty-four having displayed an aptitude in painting at least the equal of his brother. John Runciman drew both on the example of Italian art and on the work of Rembrandt. Adapting this latter style he painted *Lear in the Storm* (1767), which looks back to the earlier 52 master while prefiguring the early-Romantic Celticism that his brother was to develop. Alexander Runciman had begun his career working for the Norie firm. His visit to Rome had been financed by Sir James Clerk of Penicuik on the understanding that on his return he would paint a major mural scheme at Penicuik House. Clerk's expectation had been a scheme of classical inspiration; what he got in 1772 was wholly inspired by James Macpherson's reinterpretation of Gaelic poetry attributed to the bard Ossian. Unfortunately this major project was destroyed in its entirety by fire in 1899 but some idea of it can be gained through preparatory drawings, for example *Ossian Singing* and *The Death of Oscar.* 51 These are supplemented by an outstanding series of etchings in which Runciman developed a vivid, gestural linearity. The broader current of artistic innovation to which Runciman's Penicuik House works relate includes a mural scheme by the Irish painter James Barry (1741–1806), *The Progress of Human Culture* (1777–84), painted for the Society of Arts in London. Presiding over Barry's vision of Elysium along with Sappho, Homer, Milton and Chaucer is, of course, Ossian. Runciman had begun to experiment with Ossianic subjects derived from Macpherson while still in Rome 53 where he was in close contact with the like-minded Swiss artist Henry Fuseli (1741–1825). Fuseli wrote of Runciman that he 'was the best painter of us in Rome' and a link can also be seen between Fuseli and Runciman's fellow Scot, John Brown (1752–87); indeed their styles are often hard to tell apart. Fuseli and Runciman initiated a shift from Enlightenment views in which reason was at least a key explanatory element to a Romanticism in which the fragmentation of the explanatory structure had become the explanation

51. (opposite above) **Alexander Runciman**, *The Blind Ossian Singing and Accompanying Himself on the Harp*. 1772. A vivid sketch interpreting Macpherson's *Ossian* for a remarkable mural scheme at Penicuik House. The murals were destroyed in 1899 but a number of sketches and related etchings survive. In due course *Ossian* provided subject matter for artists throughout Europe, and was turned to again in Scotland during the Celtic revival of the 1890s.

52. (opposite below) **John Runciman** *King Lear in the Storm*, 1767. Highly regarded as a painter, Alexander Runciman's brother, John, died in Rome in his mid-twenties. In this work he shows an ability to reinterpret the lessons of Rembrandt for the beginning of the Romantic period.

itself. It is a plain shift from exploring conscious or at least explicable motives towards the exploration of the unconscious. Of his 1774 novel *The Sorrows of Young Werther*, Goethe remarked that Werther praised Homer while sane and Ossian while mad, a statement that reflects a shift in European consciousness away from the intellectual confidence of the Enlightenment.

In due course a wider European Ossianism took hold. Napoleon carried a copy of *Ossian* with him on his campaigns. Among artists it can be seen in works by Girodet (1767–1824), Runge (1777–1810) and Ingres (1780–1867). *Ossian* is also echoed by William Blake (1757–1827), both in the style of his writings and in his conception of Job as a bard, although it should be stressed that Macpherson did not provide the only 'bard' model. But what gave *Ossian* such a powerful resonance in Scotland and in Europe? On the one hand James Macpherson was a man of the Enlightenment, trained at Aberdeen University for the Ministry, interested along with his contemporaries in the origins of society and human conduct. On the other, he was a Gaelic-speaking Highlander whose clan had been Jacobite during the '45. Born in 1736 Macpherson's early life was thus an introduction to cultural contradiction. At the time he wrote *Ossian* in the 1760s his own Highland culture was being punitively dismembered in the wake of the Jacobite rebellions. What Macpherson managed to convey was a response to his own ideological fragmentation at a time when Europe was itself beginning to fragment ideologically. His significance for Scottish art is that through Alexander Runciman he began a process of Celtic revival which found its most developed expression over a century later in the Glasgow of Charles Rennie Mackintosh and the Edinburgh of Patrick Geddes.

53. **Alexander Runciman** *Fingal and Conban-cârgla*, c. 1772. Runciman's importance as an etcher is still not fully appreciated. Here his fluid use of the medium produces one of the most evocative of all illustrations of Macpherson.

Chapter 5: Art and Philosophy

Henry Raeburn and Alexander Nasmyth

The 1780s saw the loss of the first great portraitist of the Scottish Enlightenment, Allan Ramsay, and the coming to maturity of the second, Henry Raeburn (1756–1823). From this decade comes a portrait by Raeburn of *James Hutton*, the geologist, but it is in the 1790s that Raeburn's real genius shines through. Raeburn seems to have had some contact with Allan Ramsay's assistant David Martin, but otherwise (and even in this respect) his education as an artist is a puzzle. He began his career as an apprentice goldsmith in Edinburgh, but he never studied at the Trustees' Academy.

54. **Henry Raeburn** *Niel Gow*, c. 1793. Raeburn creates an enduring icon of Scottish musicianship in this portrait of a fiddler whose music is still played today. Niel Gow is shown as he no doubt was, an unpretentious man and an authoritative musician.

55. (opposite) **Henry Raeburn** *Sir John and Lady Clerk of Penicuik*, 1791–92. Here Raeburn makes of reflected light a visual metaphor for the sympathy, the mutual recognition of shared humanity, that Adam Smith considered fundamental to social relations.

However, he certainly knew Alexander Runciman, then Master of the Trustees' Academy and took some lessons from him independently. In due course he met Reynolds in London while en route for Italy, where he was in the company of the elderly Gavin Hamilton. But he does not seem to have been greatly influenced by these experiences except in so far as year by year he showed a growing confidence in his handling of paint and a growing appreciation of masters such as Velasquez. Thus although one can relate Raeburn to his predecessors and contemporaries, one must concede to him a genuine independence of vision, never better demonstrated than in *Sir John and Lady Clerk of Penicuik* (1791–92). This work is both a brilliant essay in the properties of reflected light and a portrait not just of two people but of a relationship. His portraits of this period of Scottish life have a wonderful immediacy, both in their application of paint and their sense of the personality of the sitter. This is clear whether he is painting the fiddler *Niel Gow* (1793) in the act of playing or

55

54

56

56. **Henry Raeburn** *Isabella McLeod, Mrs James Gregory*, 1798. With a confident application of paint which seems almost relaxed, Raeburn's ability to convey the appearance and character of his sitters is seen very clearly in works such as this.

Isabella McLeod (1798) in the radiance of early adulthood. Raeburn was a more private person than Ramsay but, like the earlier painter he was on close terms with the philosophers of Edinburgh. Among his friends was Dugald Stewart, who had succeeded Adam Ferguson as Professor of Moral Philosophy at the University of Edinburgh. Stewart was a follower of Thomas Reid and one of Raeburn's finest portraits, which now hangs in Fyvie Castle, shows Reid in 1796, the year of his death. In the context of Raeburn's painting in general it is interesting to note, as Duncan Macmillan has pointed out, that Thomas Reid was an early exponent of the idea of perception as a constructive mental process which assembled a pattern of sensed tone and colour into a meaningful image. These ideas resonate with the tonal-mosaic approach to paint that Raeburn takes in his portraiture from the 1790s onwards. The point is not that Raeburn had studied Reid's works, although he may have, but that he was part of a milieu in which the nature of perception was discussed and that such discussion had an effect on his practice. One of Raeburn's most well-known paintings, *Colonel Alasdair Macdonell of Glengarry* (1811), is a rather different sort of exercise in visual philosophy. At first sight it is a straightforward updating of a type of image painted by John Michael Wright, Richard Waitt, William Mosman and others. On closer inspection it is an ambivalent image in which Raeburn explores the same paradoxes of cultural loss and survival addressed by James Macpherson. Raeburn took the established tradition of full-length portraits in Highland dress and remade it in the light of the failed Jacobite project. The conceptual shift is from tartan as something to wear to tartan as something to dress up in. Much of the painting is given over to shadow but this is no longer the clear shadow of Allan's *Origin of Painting*; rather it is an indistinct shadow of a confusing past. In evoking this ambiguity Raeburn caught the character of the person he was painting very accurately. This particular chief was renowned both for his spectacular commitment to Highland dress and for the mismanagement of his estates which forced many of his clan to emigrate to Canada. Another aspect of Raeburn's remaking of the portrait in Highland dress is found in earlier works such as *Sir John Sinclair of Ulbster* (c. 1795), in which the new role of tartan as a confident British military accessory is clear.

Among Raeburn's contemporaries Archibald Skirving (1749–1819) must be mentioned. Famous for his red-chalk version of Nasmyth's portrait of Burns, he was one of the outstanding painters in pastel of his day. Notable works in that medium include

57
58

57. **Henry Raeburn** *Thomas Reid*, 1796. Raeburn painted most of the scientists and philosophers of his day, including James Hutton and Adam Ferguson, but this portrait of Thomas Reid is one of his finest. It is quite probable that Reid's theoretical distinction between sensation and perception was a direct influence on Raeburn in the development of his technique.

58. (opposite) **Henry Raeburn** *Colonel Alasdair Macdonell of Glengarry*, 1811. Although overused as an icon of uncritical Scottishness, this work can be read as a commentary on the failed Jacobite project, of which Raeburn's father had himself been part.

Prof' Thomas Reid, D.D.

portraits of Gavin Hamilton and John Clerk of Eldin. The portrait painters who followed Raeburn included George Watson (1767–1837), who trained in Reynolds' studio in London and became first president of the nascent Scottish Academy in 1826. His nephew John Watson Gordon (1788–1864) followed the path of his uncle as president of the (by then Royal) Scottish Academy in 1850. While Raeburn painted the portraits by which Sir Walter Scott is remembered, John Watson Gordon's works include valuable likenesses of other writers of the day, for instance James Hogg and the poet Lady Nairne. A few years younger was John Zephaniah Bell (1794–1883), one of the most individual painters of his age. Born in Dundee, he maintained strong links with that city but educated himself at the Royal Academy schools in London. He also studied in Paris at the studio of Baron Gros, and in this he was a forerunner of the Paris education which became commonplace for Scottish painters towards the end of the nineteenth century. Subsequently he studied

59. Alexander Nasmyth
Castle Huntly and the Tay,
c. 1800. Following the example
of the Norie family and Jacob
More, in the decades either side
of the beginning of the nineteenth
century Nasmyth painted works
which successfully unite the
principles of ideal landscape
found in Claude with the real
topography of Scotland.

in Rome and was influenced by the Nazarenes to experiment
with fresco back in Scotland.

The one portrait which Raeburn might have been expected to
paint was that of his near contemporary Robert Burns (1759–96),
but the poet's face is remembered instead through the image painted
in 1787 by Alexander Nasmyth (1758–1840). Nasmyth is a figure
of great interest. He and Burns were close friends, sharing radical
political views. They also had a common curiosity about the development of technology and in 1788 both men were on board the
maiden voyage on Dalswinton Loch in Ayrshire of Patrick Miller's
experimental steamboat. Nasmyth had himself acted as draftsman
for the project but his engineering talent only finds full expression
in the work of his son James (1808–90), inventor of that key tool of

heavy industry, the steam hammer. In this context of art and engineering it is worth noting the strength of the geometrical tradition in Scotland in the eighteenth and nineteenth centuries. As George Davie has pointed out in *The Democratic Intellect*, this training in visual thinking was defended against the newer technique of algebra on the grounds that is was a philosophically more rewarding method of mathematics. As such it was part of the intellectual heritage of every Scottish artist, architect and engineer. Alexander Nasmyth's major contribution was to the painting of Scottish landscape both rural and urban. David Wilkie called him the father of Scottish landscape painting. Nasmyth studied at the Trustees' Academy under Runciman (whose occasional landscapes would have influenced him) before going on to work with

59

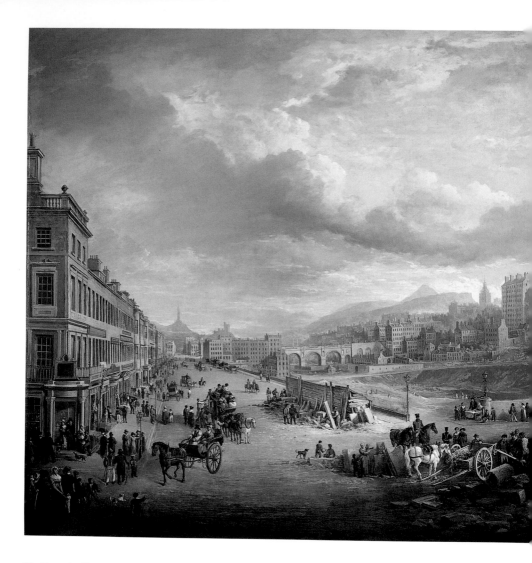

61. Alexander Nasmyth
Edinburgh from Princes Street with the Commencement of the Building of the Royal Institution, 1825. An exploration of the urban landscape of Scotland during a time of change. The edge of the classical New Town of Edinburgh is counterpointed by the Old Town and the exposed geology beyond. At the heart of the composition, the first purpose-built institution for the support of art in Scotland is under construction.

Ramsay in London. In due course he travelled to Italy where he visited Jacob More in Rome and on his return to Scotland one finds him committed to a classically informed vision. At this time the formulator of the 'rules' of the picturesque, the English clergyman William Gilpin, was publishing his work, a process begun in 1782 and completed in 1809. Nasmyth would certainly have been aware of those writings. Complementing these influences was both an awareness of Northern European landscape painting, in particular Hobbema and Ruysdael, and an awareness of the relevance of Scottish literature to landscape. Allan Ramsay senior's *Gentle*

Shepherd with its specific location in the Pentland Hills had been published in 1725. James Thomson's poem cycle *The Seasons* followed in 1729. Within its extraordinary geographical, historical and mythological scope the poet's Scottish origins can be felt, not least in lines which seem to refer to the Falls of Clyde, the subject upon which Jacob More based his reputation and a subject painted also by Nasmyth. Ramsay and Thomson thus provide a literary context for the development of what one might call a school of national landscape in Scotland, to echo a description of More's *Falls of Clyde* works by the Edinburgh art teacher George Walker. As Nasmyth's biographer J. C. B. Cooksey has pointed out, writing in 1807 Walker referred to these as 'national works' and this association of landscape and nation is of considerable interest. It was given later expression by Ruskin in *The Two Paths* and an early formulation by the ballad collector David Herd in his *Ancient and Modern Scottish Songs* (1769). By 1790 it had become a key principle in Archibald Alison's *Essays on Taste*. Alison was a near contemporary of Nasmyth and his work can be seen as an aspect of the eighteenth-century concern with perception as a constructive process. This is particularly relevant to landscape painting for in Alison's view the painter's role was to associate nature and culture. Alison writes of the ability of the mind to bestow upon external objects: 'a character which does not belong to them; and even with the rudest or common appearances of nature, to connect feelings of a nobler or a more interesting kind, than any that the mere influences of matter can ever convey.'

Architecture can mediate such associations and Nasmyth's occasional buildings exemplify this. In 1789 he designed the temple of St Bernard's Well by the Water of Leith in Edinburgh. On the one hand this structure evokes the temples to be found in the paintings of Claude, on the other it is a woodland echo of the radical urban simplicity of Adam's mausoleum for David Hume built over a decade earlier in 1777. That work by Adam became the focus of a later painting by Nasmyth, *Edinburgh from Calton Hill* (1825), which together with its companion, *Princes Street with the Commencement of the Building of the Royal Institution* (1825), comprises a remarkable urban analysis. The former work looks west into the city from the crags of Calton Hill. The latter looks east to the slopes of Arthur's Seat from the the heart of Princes Street. In each case the interrelationship of the organic medievalism of the Old Town and the utopian vision of the New Town, then in the process of construction, is clearly stated. The wider relationship between the city as a whole and the natural rock upon which it is

61

62. **John Knox** *Landscape with Tourists at Loch Katrine*, c. 1820. Owing much to the visual language of Nasmyth, this is an early response to Sir Walter Scott's poem, *The Lady of the Lake*. The key elements of the tourist industry are already in place, even down to the piper.

founded is equally clear, reminding one that James Hutton's revolutionary *Theory of the Earth* (1796) had been published, with illustrations by Nasmyth's older contemporary John Clerk of Eldin (1728–1812) not long before. At the same time Nasmyth's own personal welcome for the Royal Institution, the first purpose built building to be devoted to art in Edinburgh, is apparent. A few years earlier Nasmyth had made stage designs for a theatrical adaptation of *Heart of Midlothian* by Sir Walter Scott (1771–1832). These designs, which date from 1820, reflect the interest shared by Scott and Nasmyth both in documenting the city as it evolved and in establishing the idea of the city as of

literary and artistic character in its own right, a logical extension of Alison's associationism. A decade later Victor Hugo secured this idea in *Notre Dame de Paris*.

Nasmyth was never Master of the Trustees' Academy but he was an important teacher, exerting a powerful influence on the next generation of Scottish painters, most of whom had some significant contact with him. Among his pupils were Andrew Wilson (1780–1840), who became Master of the Trustees' Academy in 1818, the talented watercolour painter Hugh William Williams (1773–1829), and the influential amateur John Thomson of Duddingston (1778–1840). Nasmyth's son Patrick (1787–1831) responded strongly to the Netherlandish tradition of landscape painting and settled in London to become a significant part of the English school. Although it is not certain that he was a pupil, Alexander Nasmyth's closest successor in terms both of rural and urban imagery was Paisley-born John Knox (1778–1845). Knox responded to Sir Walter Scott's literary geography of Scotland in a way deferential to the Claudian tradition of Nasmyth. This can be seen in *Landscape with Tourists at Loch Katrine* painted in the 1820s, a direct visual commentary on the growing popularity of the Trossachs as a result of the publication of Scott's *The Lady of the Lake* in 1810. At the same time one finds an echo of Nasmyth's engineering interests in *The First Steam Boat on the Clyde* (1820), in which the tiny image of Henry Bell's *Comet* is placed in a frame of trees worthy of a seventeenth-century painter in Rome. Nasmyth was of course still active and works such as Knox's *The Trongate, Glasgow* (*c.* 1826) complement the older artist's contemporary urban analyses of Edinburgh. In due course Knox was to move away from his Nasmythian starting point to make panoramic works of the view from the top of Ben Lomond. These works take in the expanse of the peaks of the western Highlands and they open the way for the further development of the idea of the Highlands as a spectacle, which was to take place in the second half of the nineteenth century.

62

Interpreting the Enlightenment: David Wilkie

Ramsay, Raeburn and Nasmyth were artists at the heart of the Scottish Enlightenment. Their work developed side by side with that of the philosophers and scientists of the age. This gives their art a specific interest but it also gives it a limitation, for no generation is able to fully explore its own achievement. It thus fell to a French philosopher of the next century, Victor Cousin (1792–1867), to begin the process of advocating the philosophy of the Scottish Enlightenment in academic terms. In visual terms such exploration was undertaken by David Wilkie (1785–1841). Wilkie is an extraordinary figure in Scottish art. He is known within the wider British tradition as the founder of the school of nineteenth-century genre painting. In terms of Scottish painting he is recognized in addition as a portrait painter and as a pioneer of the interpretation of Scottish history which was to be such a significant trend in the latter part of the century. He defines his generation by drawing together the developments of the eighteenth century and extending and amplifying them for the new century. The philosophers of the Enlightenment were interested in the nature of perception, the nature of the self, the nature of society and the nature of history and they helped to lay the foundations for what we now call the social sciences. It is this social scientific territory that Wilkie explored in art. Speaking at a dinner in his honour in Rome in 1827, he reflected on the interdependence of ideas and art when he commented that 'no art that is not intellectual can be worthy of Scotland'.

Born in Fife, the son of a Presbyterian minister, Wilkie attended the Trustees' Academy as early as 1799 and in Edinburgh he came into contact with both Nasmyth and Raeburn. Like his contemporaries Alexander Carse (c. 1770–1843), John Burnet (1784–1868) and James Howe (1780–1836), he was deeply impressed by David Allan's work, in particular the illustrations for Allan Ramsay's *Gentle Shepherd*. In his twentieth year he showed his quality and range as an artist. *The Chalmers Bethune Family* (1804), even more than Raeburn's *Sir John and Lady Clerk of Penicuik*, conveys the nature of a relationship or rather a set of relationships. Wilkie paints this family as a totality, that is to say he shows the way each member relates to every other and the way they relate to him as an artist. Another remarkable early work influenced by Alexander Carse, *Pitlessie Fair* (1804), extends this social theme while making clear his interest in the Dutch genre tradition. Its success enabled Wilkie to move to London to study at the Royal Academy. London was to be his base for the rest of his career but, as with Ramsay, the Scottish intellectual tradition was always his point of reference. Works such as the *Village Politicians* (1806) and *The Blind Fiddler* (1806) can be read as visual manifestos of the pioneering medical study of human expression by the Edinburgh surgeon and anatomist Charles Bell (1774–1842). Wilkie contributed an illustration to Bell's *The Anatomy of Expression in Painting*, published in 1806, and it should be noted that Bell was himself a fine draughtsman, having trained with David Allan. As

63. **David Wilkie** *The Chalmers Bethune Family*, 1804. Wilkie painted this perceptive family portrait before he was twenty. It is worthy of Raeburn yet takes the older artist's exploration of character and social relations onto a new level of intimacy between painter and sitters.

63

55

66

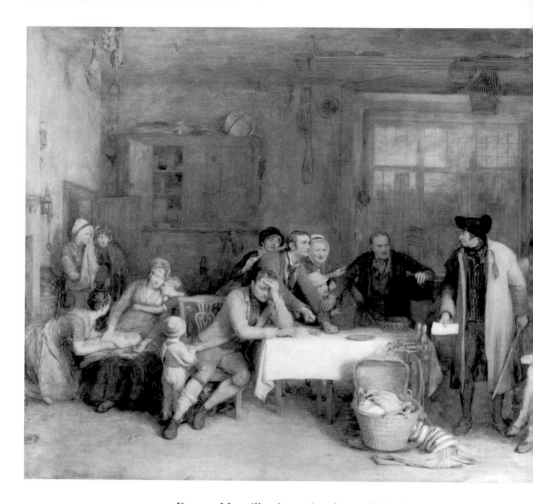

Duncan Macmillan has pointed out, this is the context for the interest shown in Wilkie's work by the French painter Théodore Géricault (1791–1824) when he visited Wilkie's studio in 1821. Wilkie's investigation of social and economic reality is illustrated by *Distraining for Rent* (1815) and *The Penny Wedding* (1818). The former is an implied critique of the landlord class and was not well received by Wilkie's patrons. *The Penny Wedding* is both a reversion to the commercially safe territory of folk-painting and a deliberate contrast to *Distraining for Rent*. Drawing on David Allan it evokes a Highland golden age of rural community and mutual support where Niel Gow still plays his fiddle.

64

Wilkie's understanding of earlier Scottish genre painting and its debt to the Netherlands was highly influential both north and south of the Border. Scottish painters directly

64. **David Wilkie** *Distraining for Rent*, 1815. Unpopular with his patrons in London for its implied criticism of the landlord class, this painting makes clear Wilkie's view of the artist as social commentator.

influenced by him at this time include, as well as John Burnet, Alexander Fraser (1785–1865), William Lizars (1788–1859), William Kidd (*c.* 1790–1863), Walter Geikie (1795–1837), and George Harvey (1806–1876). A later generation which included John Phillip (1817–67), Erskine Nicol (1825–1904) and the brothers John (1818–1902) and Thomas Faed (1826–1900) took Wilkie-influenced genre paintings into the second half of the nineteenth century, although by then the late-Enlightenment project on which Wilkie himself was engaged had been forgotten. Linda Colley has recognized Wilkie's perceptiveness by drawing attention to his painting *The Chelsea Pensioners reading the Gazette of the Battle of Waterloo* (1822) as a discourse on the complex nature of a British identity brought into focus by the Napoleonic Wars. Wilkie's 1822 sketch of *The Preaching of Knox before the Lords of the Congregation, 10 July, 1559* can be considered a cognate reflection on the pluralistic nature of Scottishness through the contrasted historical and psychological positions of John Knox and Mary Queen of Scots. Such cultural and ideological comparison is at the heart of Wilkie's art and he lost no time in travelling to France, Italy and Spain as soon as the end of the Napoleonic wars allowed. The success of his Spanish work encouraged both David Roberts and later John Phillip to explore that country. At the same time Wilkie continued to develop specifically Scottish aspects of his work including illustrations to the poems and songs of Robert Burns which culminate in his Rembrandt-like *The Cotter's Saturday Night* (1837). His last journey was to Turkey and the Holy Land to observe the culture of the Ottoman Empire and see for himself the

65

65. **David Wilkie** *The Preaching of Knox before the Lords of the Congregation, 10 July, 1559*, 1822. A sketch for a work only completed a decade later, this is a key image in the development of the representation of Scottish history in art. The son of a Presbyterian minister himself, Wilkie treats Knox with fascination and Mary Queen of Scots with sympathy, in a way that has characterized the view of these figures ever since.

66. David Wilkie *The Blind Fiddler*, 1806. Rather than merely anecdotal in its subject matter, this painting shows Wilkie beginning to engage with the philosophical concerns of the Scottish Enlightenment both societal and perceptual. The comparison of relative poverty is clear enough; what is less obvious is Wilkie's exploration of the varieties of representation with reference to imitation, self-portraiture and children's drawing.

sites of Biblical events. In these works one finds an appreciation of other cultures, a respect for religious observance and above all a sense of shared humanity. He observed the life of Jerusalem or Istanbul just as he had observed the life of Fife or Italy or Spain. Had he not died at sea on his homeward journey, it may be that the exoticism which came to define Orientalism in Britain would have been counterbalanced by his careful and sympathetic cultural anthropology. It is Wilkie's integrity of vision that led J. M.W. Turner, his great rival at the Royal Academy in London, to paint *Peace, Burial at Sea* (1842) as his memorial.

The careers of Ramsay, Raeburn, Nasmyth and Wilkie consolidated the achievement of earlier painters. The need for a representative body for Scottish artists was now pressing and in 1826 a group formed themselves into the Scottish Academy. This was in part a reaction to the formation in 1819 of the Institution for the Encouragement of Fine Arts in Scotland as a body to present exhibitions. That organization had rapidly lost credibility by excluding practising artists from its decision-making in favour of a board described by Esmé Gordon, the historian of the Academy, as 'a body of autocratic, aristocratic men'. The scene was set for a number of tussles between the two bodies. The situation was sorted out with the help of the distinguished lawyer Lord Cockburn by what was in effect (although not in principle) a merger. In due course in 1835 the Royal Institution building on Princes Street became the home of Scottish Academy exhibitions but it was seventy-five years before the name of the building itself was changed to 'The Royal Scottish Academy', the Royal Charter having been given 1837. It should also be noted that the members of the Royal Scottish Academy were seminal in the establishment of the National Gallery of Scotland, which opened to the public in 1859.

Towards a National School of Sculpture
This same period saw the vigorous development of portrait sculpture in Scotland. While facilities for painters had been improving in the second half of the eighteenth century, educational facilities for sculptors were still lacking. Major commissions were routinely given to London-based sculptors such as John Flaxman (1755–1826) and Francis Chantrey (1771–1841); for example, Flaxman made the figure of Burns for the inside of the classical monument in Edinburgh designed in the poet's honour by Thomas Hamilton and erected in 1830. One of the earliest sculptors of this tradition to be active in Scotland itself was the English sculptor Samuel

67. **Lawrence Macdonald**
George Combe, c. 1830.
Macdonald was a key figure in the establishment of sculpture as an independent discipline in early nineteenth-century Scotland. Here he portrays the psychologist and phrenologist, George Combe.

Joseph (1791–1850) who worked in Edinburgh from 1821–29. Joseph had trained at the Royal Academy in London and although he stayed less than ten years north of the Border he was highly-regarded by his fellow artists and was a founder member of the Scottish Academy. Among many notable works he made remarkable heads in marble of the philosopher Dugald Stewart and of Henry Mackenzie, author of the influential short novel *The Man of Feeling*. Much later he made a posthumous bust of David Wilkie (1842). This image of the tousle-haired painter gazing into the distance shows Joseph at his best, echoing Bernini and participating in the Romanticism of the age. Edinburgh-born Thomas Campbell (*c.* 1790–1858) solved the problem posed by lack of facilities in Scotland by studying at the Royal Academy in London a few years after Joseph. Thereafter he settled in Rome where, after Canova's death in 1822, he received significant commissions from British patrons such as the sixth Duke of Devonshire. He set up a studio in London in 1830 and among other notable works designed the Hopetoun Memorial (1824–34) in St Andrew Square in Edinburgh and the memorial to Sarah Siddons in Westminster Abbey in London. A few years younger than Campbell, Lawrence Macdonald (1799–1878), having first studied briefly at the Trustees' Academy, also studied in Rome and, like Campbell, he was successful there. Back in Edinburgh from 1827 he followed closely on Samuel Joseph's heels first as an associate and then as a member of the new Scottish Academy. In 1832 he returned to Rome and worked there for the rest of his life. He is remembered not least for his impressive portrait of General Sir David Baird, which was used by Wilkie as the model for his painting of *Sir David Baird Discovering the Body of Sultan Tippoo Sahib* (1839). Among Macdonald's finest works is a bust of his friend the phrenologist George Combe (*c.* 1830). The theory of phrenology, which relates bumps on the skull to character, had immediate interest for Macdonald as a portrait sculptor. Although this theory was wrong, it was wrong in an interesting way for it was a step on the road to the idea of localization of brain function. George Combe was thus a scientist of note and along with his brother Andrew he laid the basis for the study of psychology at the University of Edinburgh. Macdonald's interest in Combe's theories was reciprocated by Combe's interest in art. This interaction of artist and scientist should be seen as part of the wider investigation of the nature of expression and emotion current in the Edinburgh of the day, which continued the explorations of Charles Bell and David Wilkie.

67

68. **William Allan** *The Slave
Market, Constantinople*, 1838.
Widely travelled in Russia and
the Middle East, Allan made an
early contribution to European
orientalism in this work. His
Scottish subjects often illustrate
scenes addressed by his friend
Sir Walter Scott in his novels.

Chapter 6:   Nineteenth-Century Narratives

Hispanicism, Orientalism and Scottish History
The Napoleonic wars disrupted the typical Rome-based art education of the Scottish artist but brought other areas into focus.
Military campaigns in the Middle East and Spain had made these
areas psychologically salient in a way that they had not been
before. Wilkie was one painter who responded to this new pattern
of influence in the 1820s and it reached its zenith a generation later
in a series of vivid paintings of Spanish street scenes by John
Phillip. Works such as his masterpiece *La Gloria: A Spanish Wake*
(1864) owe something to Wilkie but in their freedom of technique
and use of colour have gone further and can be considered as outstanding examples of High Victorian subject paintings. Phillip's
response to the intensity of southern European light prefigures
the work of Arthur Melville in the 1880s and is thus a link between
the world of Wilkie and late nineteenth-century developments.
This Scottish interest in Spain was also expressed in terms of art
criticism, for the first major critical account of Spanish painting in
the English language was written by Phillip's close contemporary, the collector William Stirling-Maxwell (1818–78). Another
artist to be influenced by the shift in pattern of artistic opportunities was David Roberts (1796–1864). In 1838–39 he had travelled
to the Holy Land and Egypt and some years before had, like   69
Wilkie, travelled extensively in Spain. Edinburgh-born Roberts
was one of the last painters to emerge from the decorator-painter
tradition and he was an experienced theatre-set painter working
in this capacity in both Edinburgh and London. Such work gave
him an understanding of architectural scale, which stood him in
good stead in his representations of the ancient architecture of the
Middle East. The dispassionate, accurate quality of Roberts's work
is complemented by a tonal subtlety evocative of place. In lithographic form his works had a wide public and they were influential
on architects such as Alexander 'Greek' Thomson (1817–75) of
Glasgow. Thomson was inspired also by the apocalyptic visions
of the English artist John Martin (1789–1854), to which some of
Roberts's early imaginary compositions can be related.

69. **David Roberts** *Thebes, Karnac*, 1838. Roberts's watercolours of Egypt and the Holy Land, convincingly composed and architecturally accurate, were a key component in creating the image of the Middle East for Victorian Britain.

Wilkie's fellow student at the Trustees' Academy, William Allan (1782–1850), found his early subject matter further afield, spending the years 1805–1814 in Russia and Turkey. He is shown dressed in Circassian gear that he had brought back from his travels in an etching made in 1815 by Andrew Geddes (1783–1844). The period was one both of fragmentation of cultural reference and of the creation of a notion of Europe through the medium of the historical novel, which in Georg Lukacs's words 'arose at the beginning of the nineteenth century at about the time of Napoleon's collapse – Scott's *Waverley* appeared in 1814'. William Allan was a friend of Scott and his paintings from the 1830s reflect this, for example *The Murder of Rizzio* (1833). Five years later Allan drew on a further visit to Turkey in *The Slave Market, Constantinople* (1838). Whereas in the earlier work his style echoes that of Wilkie, the latter work shows a keen awareness of the activities of early French orientalists such as Vernet (1789–1863) and Decamps (1803–60). Among Allan's contemporaries was the influential antiquary David Laing (1793–1878) and the linkage of antiquarianism and exoticism which finds full expression in Scott's novels on the one hand and Allan's paintings on the other should be noted. Allan was highly influential, not least through his teaching as Master of the Trustees' Academy and his presidency of the Royal Scottish Academy.

Advances in landscape painting were being made by John Thomson of Duddingston (1778–1840). Many of his paintings interpret the spirit of place of Scott's works and can be considered a sort of landscape counterpart to the figurative approach of William Allan. Thomson studied with Nasmyth but he developed a vision of landscape conveyed with heavy impasto which finds its most powerful expression in rugged coastal scenes such as *Fast Castle from Below* (c. 1824). These works are rarely wholly successful but they are important experiments. They betray the amateur

status of the artist – Thomson was a Minister of the Church of Scotland – but they also remind one of his friendship with J. M.W. Turner. The latter's contribution to literary illustration is often overlooked and while Turner's work is outside the scope of this book his strong bond to Sir Walter Scott just before the author's death should not go unacknowledged. His illustrations for the 1833 edition of Scott's poetry have an elegiac quality and his views of the Highlands avoid the simplistic imagery of his compatriot Landseer twenty years later. Many of these watercolours were engraved by the Edinburgh artist and steel-engraver William Miller (1796–1882), considered by Ruskin to be Turner's best interpreter in that medium. Miller is himself a figure of considerable interest. He was present at the first meeting of the Scottish Academy in 1826 and he has the further distinction of having engraved images for David Octavius Hill in the 1830s before Hill turned to the newly invented printmaking technique of photography in the 1840s.

Painting, Religion, Photography

In the works that both Wilkie and Allan painted on the theme of the life of Mary Queen of Scots they took further the experiments of Gavin Hamilton and John Alexander in the previous century. At the same time they set the course that this art illustrating the drama of Scottish history would follow. Integral to it are the figures of Knox and Mary, contrasted in ideology, in religion and in gender. These distinctions give form and tension to the imagery that developed. Three related strands can be distinguished in due course: the conflict of Knox and Mary itself, the tribulations of the Covenanters, and the tribulations of the Jacobites. The main periods addressed are firstly the Reformation of the 1560s, secondly – and consequent on the unresolved matters of the Reformation – the 'killing time' of the 1680s which saw the supression of Presbyterian Covenanters, and thirdly the years of 1745 and 1746 which saw the final failure of the Roman Catholic and Episcopalian Jacobites to regain power. These paintings reflect a crucial phase in the articulation of modern Scottish identity. The same artists painted ideologically and religiously opposed Covenanters and Jacobites with equal commitment. Such works thus articulate the interplay of cultural contradictions which is found not only in the historical background of modern Scotland but is often equally obvious in the family histories of individual Scots. The linking themes in these works are not so much historical facts as historical processes, namely oppression, resistance and

71. **Thomas Duncan** *The Death of John Brown of Priesthill*, 1844. Duncan helped to create a romanticized imagery of Covenanter struggle, which parallels and complements the imagery of Jacobite struggle developed during the same period.

cultural survival. Awareness of these processes helped to delineate Scottishness both in a post-Union context and in the context of the new strength of a British identity associated with the growing Empire. In this sense the oppositional themes are often more important than the overt content of the works. Jacobites and Covenanters may represent opposed ideologies but they can be united by struggle even if their struggle is potentially against one another. These works both reflect and contribute to the development of a pluralist cultural nationalism in Scotland in the nineteenth century. But equally important in some paintings is the overt use of history to inform contemporary events. This is particularly true of those works with Covenanter subjects painted in the period leading up to the Disruption of the Church of Scotland in 1843. This was a major schism within the main body of Scottish Presbyterianism, which continued for the best part of a century. It was caused by disagreement about the relative powers of church and state, broadly speaking the same issue that had led to the signing of the National Covenant two centuries earlier, so works depicting Covenanters had a particular resonance. Paintings such as George Harvey's *The Covenanters Preaching* (1830), William Allan's *The Signing of the National Covenant in Greyfriars Kirkyard* (c. 1840), *The Marriage of the Covenanter* (1842) by Alexander Johnston (1815–91), and Thomas Duncan's *The Death of John Brown of Priesthill* (1844) must be seen in that light.

71

72. **Robert Scott Lauder** *Christ Teacheth Humility*, 1847. An appreciation of old masters is clear in this work, and Lauder was to pass on his profound knowledge of European art to his students at the Trustees' Academy in Edinburgh in the 1850s.

73. (opposite) **William Dyce** *Christ As The Man of Sorrows*, 1860. Dyce creates here an extraordinary synthesis of Christian belief and Highland landscape. Faith is brought home, literally. The point is repeated for the Old Testament in a companion work, *David in the Wilderness*.

The same period saw, for the first time since the Reformation, the development of imagery directly based on biblical events, for example *Christ Teacheth Humility* (1847) by John Thomson's son-in-law, Robert Scott Lauder (1803–61). This was a proposal for a mural in the new Houses of Parliament in London and it was submitted to one of a series of exhibitions held in Westminster Hall which were an important stimulus to the artists of the time. Lauder's work united the influence of Wilkie, not least his unfinished *Knox Administering the Sacrament at Calder House* (1839), with the lighter, more Mediterranean palette of Roberts, all in the overall context of an appreciation of Rembrandt and Rubens. Robert Scott Lauder also made an impression in London with a number of paintings illustrating scenes from Scott's Waverley novels and was in demand as portrait painter. He was one of a remarkable group of artists born between 1800 and 1815. It included David Octavius Hill (1802–70), Horatio McCulloch (1805–67), David Scott (1806–49), George Harvey (1806–76), William Dyce (1806–64), Daniel Macnee (1806–82), Thomas Duncan (1807–45), William Bell Scott (1811–90), James Eckford Lauder (1811–69) and the sculptor John Steell (1804–91). Apart from the fact that they all belonged to the nascent Scottish Academy, there is no common thread in their careers but their interest lies in their very variety.

Lauder's proposal for the new Houses of Parliament was unsuccessful but in the event much of the mural work went to Aberdeen-born William Dyce who had been brought in to advise on the competition by Prince Albert. Dyce imbued his work with the influence of Italian Renaissance painting gained at first hand, for by 1825 Italy had again assumed its former importance in the education of Scottish artists. He was strongly influenced by Venetian art and in Rome the example of the German Nazarene painters was of great importance to him, both in terms of the clarity of outline they insisted upon and in their revival of fresco as a technique appropriate to the nineteenth century. Most of Dyce's career was spent in London where he was a respected teacher and administrator, having a key role in the development of art education in England as superintendent of the Government Schools of Design. It was Dyce who introduced John Ruskin to the art of the Pre-Raphaelites and he was the main link between the Nazarenes and those like-minded English artists. Dyce's support for Pre-Raphaelitism came to be reflected in his own works which in the 1850s became more Pre-Raphaelite in style, truer in a detailed sense to nature. This reaches a high point in *Christas the Man of*

Sorrows and its companion piece *David in the Wilderness*, both from 1860. Yet although these paintings are Pre-Raphaelite in their sensitivity to detail, Dyce's setting goes against the tenets of Pre-Raphaelitism, which insisted on truth in all things including historical location, for Christ and David are placed on Highland moorland. Dyce literally brings home to Scotland the central figures of the Old and New Testaments and the religious power of the paintings is increased by their geographical immediacy. There is an echo here of a passage from *The Two Paths* (1858) in which Ruskin – who was himself a Scot by family background – identifies closeness to nature with moral virtue using the conditions of life in the Highlands to support his rhetoric. Dyce's *Pegwell Bay, Kent – A Recollection of October 5th 1858* is widely regarded as the archetypal Pre-Raphaelite landscape. Finished in 1860 it shows a precise moment in the lives of Dyce's family put into perspective both geological and cosmic by the cliffs behind them and Donati's Comet in the sky above. In a work of some years before, *Shirrapburn Loch* (*c.* 1855), one finds in Dyce an intriguing echo of the classical landscape formula of Alexander Nasmyth united with a Pre-Raphaelite attention to detail.

Where Dyce echoes Nasmyth only as a very occasional part of a wider artistic language, in the work of David Octavius Hill one finds a systematic reworking of Nasmyth's interests. Like Nasmyth's follower John Knox but a generation younger, Hill was committed to the visual and intellectual possibilities offered by the urban and rural topography of Scotland. And like Nasmyth himself he was committed to the poetry of Burns. Hill was born in Perth and studied at the Trustees' Academy with Andrew Wilson. A central figure in the Edinburgh art world of the time, he acted as secretary of the Royal Scottish Academy from its early years until his death in 1870. In his paintings of Edinburgh the Enlightenment clarity of the city of Nasmyth re-emerges softened by a Turnerian light. Among his achievements was an extraordinary visual tribute to Robert Burns, comprising over thirty images that were engraved and published as *The Land of Burns* (1840), together with essays by Professor John Wilson and Robert Chambers. Both David Allan and David Wilkie had made major contributions to the imagery developing around the life and works of Burns but these were for the most part genre scenes based on the poems and songs. Hill's approach to the poet through landscape often results in works of expressive verve which echo Turner's involvement with the works of Scott a few years earlier, but the dominant influence for Hill is still Claude by way of Nasmyth. There are also genre

75

74. **David Octavius Hill and Robert Adamson** *Mrs Elizabeth (Johnstone) Hall, c.* 1844. The pioneering photographic work of Hill and Adamson in the 1840s was both an extension of Wilkie's interest in the nature of society and a precursor of modern documentary photography.

scenes which draw, via Wilkie, on a Netherlandish tradition, and one remarkable fantasy image, *The Poet's Dream*. The latter, by uniting within a single image an Ossian-like bard and a classical monument to the poet, reminds one of the complementarity between Celticism and classicism in the poetry of Burns and in Scottish thought in general.

Hill's reputation today is based almost exclusively on the pioneering photographic work which he carried out in conjunction with the chemist Robert Adamson (1821–48). The continued interest in his record of the Disruption of the Church of Scotland in 1843, *Signing the Act of Separation and the Deed of Demission* (1843–67) relates to this. It stems largely from the fact that at the prompting of the physicist David Brewster, Hill recognized the potential of the new art of photography as an aid in recording the features of the multitude of ministers and radical thinkers who had seceded from the Church of Scotland. One of the finest of these calotype portraits was of the stone mason, geologist and journalist

74

75. **David Octavius Hill** *A View of Edinburgh from North of the Castle, showing the Castle, the New Town and the Firth of Forth,* 1859 or after. Hill's ability as an artist has been overshadowed by his achievement as a photographer. Here he remakes Nasmyth's urban vision in the light of Turner.

Hugh Miller who wrote the earliest account of this photographic project. (Calotype, a negative process invented by William Henry Fox Talbot, became obsolete after ten years.) The wider documentary and aesthetic possibilities were immediately apparent. In a letter of July 1843 David Brewster had written to his friend Fox Talbot: 'I think you will find that we have, in Scotland, found out the value of your invention not before yourself, but before those to

whom you have given the privilege of using it.' Soon after this Hill
and Adamson began their magnificent series of calotypes of the
fisher folk of Newhaven which have in due course gained acknowledgment from commentators as contrasted as Alfred Stieglitz
and Walter Benjamin. These works are both clear successors of
Wilkie's genre paintings and precursors of the documentary
photo-essays taken for granted today.

Wilderness as Backdrop

The more direct response to landscape found in John Knox's *Ben Lomond* panoramas was taken forward by an artist who was probably his student, Glasgow-born Horatio McCulloch. With McCulloch, Scottish landscape enters a period of transition from the classicism of Nasmyth to the early modern experiments of William McTaggart and the Glasgow School. The form that this transition took was a pictorialism that prefigures the postcard image of the Highlands. But just as a postcard shows reality, if selectively, so did McCulloch, and his slightly exaggerated dramatic grasp of Highland land-masses in works like *Glencoe* (1864) still impresses today. Whatever its visual merits, McCulloch's work was part of a process of distancing the relationship of people to land in the Highlands. In the Victorian period the Highlands

76

began to be defined as a wilderness instead of a populated space and many communities were cleared from the land in favour of large sheep farms and sporting interests. Symbolic of this was the rebuilding of Balmoral Castle in the 1850s as a holiday home for Queen Victoria and Prince Albert, its surrounding wildlife immortalized in Landseer's *The Monarch of the Glen* (1851). By the 1860s the main elements of the tartan, heather and hills stereotype of modern Scotland were in place, the irony being that this stereotype was based on an area of Scotland which was being systematically depopulated. That stereotype was maintained through holiday visits increasingly available to people throughout Britain, but the same railways that made this possible enabled journalists to have greater awareness of the Clearances, which thus then became matters of public consciousness. Despite the ambiguities of his work when viewed from today's perspective McCulloch shared this awareness, for one of his best-known paintings engages with the Clearances, if in an oblique fashion. It was initially entitled *The Emigrant's Dream of His Highland Home* (1860) and it is an imaginary and evocative landscape of lochs and mountains. It was retitled *My Heart's in the Highlands* when it appeared as an illustration of Burns' eponymous poem, engraved by William Forrest. At one and the same time the tourist is enticed and the memory of the emigrant is engaged. A few years later what is perhaps the most famous image of the Clearances, *The Last of the Clan* (1865), was painted by Thomas Faed. Along with his elder brother John, Thomas Faed had studied at the Trustees' Academy,

76. **Horatio McCulloch** *Glencoe*, 1864. Drawing on the later panoramas of his teacher John Knox, Horatio McCulloch provided the template of the Highland painting for the Victorian age.

77. (right) **Thomas Faed** *The Last of the Clan*, 1865. One of a family of painters, all of whom were distinguished as illustrators, Thomas Faed provided a genre accompaniment to McCulloch's Highland landscapes in this painting. It shows a clansman, too old to emigrate, left on the quayside as his friends and family sail from Scotland.

but by the mid-1850s was well settled in London developing a brand of post-Wilkie genre painting of Scottish subjects of unchallenging nature. *The Last of the Clan* is something of an exception to this and it is one of a wider set of images which includes John Watson Nicol's (1856–1926) *Lochaber No More* (1883). Faed's painting, even if it does not question the Clearances, at least draws a sentimental attention to them. In its directly illustrative nature it is very similar in feel to McCulloch's work. Between them McCulloch and Faed fully exploited this seam of straightforward, illustrative painting and it is in this context that a developing crisis in the relationship between the Scottish artist and Scottish reality must be seen. This uncertainty of direction was the Scottish expression of the wider European crisis concerning the nature of representation and the role of the artist. In France it led to Impressionism. In Scotland it led to the work of William McTaggart and in his wake the Glasgow School of painters led by W. Y. Macgregor and James Guthrie.

Looking Inward: David Scott and William Bell Scott

As if to give balance to the reportage of places and events characteristic of McCulloch and Faed, these middle years of the nineteenth century also saw a psychological turning inward in Scottish art, marked in the first instance by the work of David Scott. In his supplementary chapter to Alexander Gilchrist's *Life of William Blake* (1863), Dante Gabriel Rossetti (1828–82) claimed David Scott as foremost among Blake's successors. Rossetti noted that the painter's father Robert Scott (1777–1841), an engraver by profession, had been one of the original subscribers to Blake's illustrations of Blair's *Grave* (1808) and that this would have given the young David access to Blake's designs from an early age. David Scott is an intriguing figure. As an etcher he was the first illustrator of Coleridge's *Rime of the Ancient Mariner*, making designs in 1831 which were published in 1837. In the same period he travelled to Italy, at times in the company of Dyce, and was himself impressed by the Nazarenes in Rome. Perhaps most importantly he saw at first hand the formal experiments in both the painting and sculpting of the figure made by Michelangelo and in this regard Scott was making the trip that Blake was never able to. On his return in the mid-1830s he began to push Scottish painting into a new phase of imaginative exploration and something of the power of his aesthetic impulse can be seen in utterly surprising works like *Puck Fleeing the Dawn* (1837), 78 which has every appearance of having been painted fifty years

78. **David Scott** *Puck Fleeing the Dawn*, 1837. Where contemporaries like McCulloch explored the landscape, David Scott turned inwards to embark on a psychological journey into myth and legend. His works in this vein include images illustrating Shakespeare (as shown here), Coleridge and Bunyan.

later. In paintings like this and the dream-like *Traitor's Gate* (1841) he parallels the psychodynamic quality of the writings of James Hogg (1770–1835), not only the Hogg of *The Private Memoirs and Confessions of a Justified Sinner* but the Hogg of *Pilgrims of the Sun* and *Kilmeny* poems of the supernatural and the faerie. Whether Scott is painting *Orestes seized by the Furies after the Murder of Clytemnestra* (1837) or *Wallace, The Defender of Scotland* (1843), there is present in his uneasy and hard-won compositions a sense of mental struggle made visible. Often he forces the picture plane close to the viewer as in *Philoctetes left in the Island of Lemnos* 79 *by the Greeks in their passage towards Troy* (1839). Such sense of struggle gives an unusual power to his illustrations for Bunyan's *Pilgrim's Progress* (published 1850). In a number of works Scott's admiration for the English artist William Etty (1787–1849) is evident and one can note that Etty was elected an honorary member of the Scottish Academy as early as 1829, while Scott himself became a member the following year.

David Scott's life was cut short at the age of forty-two. His younger brother William Bell Scott (1811–90) was also a talented painter and both brothers had been trained as engravers by their father at the Trustees' Academy. William Bell Scott had shown an interest in illustration of Arthurian legend in the 1830s and 1840s, and went on to paint works of legendary, historical and spiritual

79. David Scott *Philoctetes left on the Island of Lemnos by the Greeks in their passage towards Troy*, 1839. Scott's works often have a deliberate uneasiness of composition which reflects the subject matter. Here the agony of Philoctetes, wounded and abandoned, spills into the viewer's space.

interest such as *Albrecht Dürer at Nürnberg* (1854) and *Una and the Lion* (1860), a subject from Spenser's *Faerie Queen*. He was a poet as well as a painter, becoming a close friend of his younger contemporary Rossetti and contributing to the pioneering Pre-Raphaelite magazine *The Germ*. He later carried out a set of murals at Penkill Castle in Ayrshire illustrating the *The King's Quair*, a late fifteenth-century poem by James I of Scotland, on which Rossetti based his own poem, *The King's Tragedy*. From 1844 Scott was director of the Newcastle School of Art and painted a series of murals for Wallington Hall depicting the history of Northumbria. One of these was *Iron and Coal* (1855–60), a reflection on the transformative power of industry which has an added interest when compared with *Work* (1852–65) by Ford Madox Brown, a more didactic but contemporary painting. Scott also helped to establish the west coast of Scotland as a destination for artists and his *Iona* painted in 1887 (based on a drawing of 1830) is among the first views of that island that can be counted part of the modern landscape tradition.

80. William Bell Scott

In the Nineteenth Century the Northumbrians show the World what can be done with IRON and COAL, 1855–60. William Bell Scott was closely linked to the Pre-Raphaelites. While he was director of Newcastle School of Art he painted this mural at Wallington Hall in Northumberland. It bears interesting comparison with *Work* (1852–65), by his younger contemporary Ford Madox Brown.

Artists and Antiquarians

William Bell Scott's interest in Iona was part of a wider movement that included the making of visual records of the work of the West Highland School of sculptors by James Drummond (1816–77). This, as we have seen, flourished from the fourteenth to the sixteenth century. These drawings from the 1860s onwards give Drummond an importance in the history of Scottish art quite independent of his considerable achievements as a painter. Drummond was a pupil of William Allan at the Trustees' Academy and like a number of his contemporaries became a fellow of the Society of Antiquaries (founded 1780). He helped to establish and curate the society's collection, which in due course became the basis of the National Museum of Antiquities and he was also an early curator of the

81. James Drummond
The Porteous Mob, 1855. A key scene from Sir Walter Scott's *Heart of Midlothian* is brought to life in Drummond's painting. Like many images of this type it was in due course issued as an engraving and found its place in homes throughout Scotland.

developing National Gallery collection. Drummond was born in Edinburgh in the house in the Old Town reputed to have been that of John Knox. His high regard for the aesthetic and social qualities of the Old Town made him an early objector to the demolition that threatened it. In his paintings the Old Town of Edinburgh was thus often part of the subject matter. He attempted to find a visual equivalent to what Sir Walter Scott had evoked in words, that is to say to give due weight to both the architectural character of the city and to its people. An example of this is *The Porteous Mob* (1855) which illustrates an event in Edinburgh history which is also the subject of one of Scott's finest descriptive passages in

Heart of Midlothian. The painting had great success in engraved form when published by the Royal Association for the Promotion of the Fine Arts in Scotland in 1862.

Drummond's antiquarianism focused him as an artist and similar perspectives are found in two fellow members of the Society of Antiquaries, Joseph Noel Paton (1821–1901) and William Fettes Douglas (1822–91). The sense of visual concentration in Paton's *Dawn: Luther at Erfurt* (1861) is extraordinary. Such detail is given 82 to the objects surrounding Luther that Luther himself risks becoming just one more object of antiquarian interest. Consistent with this was Paton's use of paint, for the finish is so smooth that the artist's brush might not have been there at all. This clarity of vision made Paton an illustrator of impressive ability and this can be seen equally in biblical and literary projects. Typical is a series published in 1860 as engravings to illustrate the 'Dowie Dens o Yarrow', a ballad first collected by Scott in his *Border Minstrelsy*. The publisher, as for Drummond's *Porteous Mob*, was the Royal Association for the Promotion of the Fine Arts in Scotland, and

82. **Joseph Noel Paton** *Dawn: Luther at Erfurt*, 1861. In works of high finish such as this, Paton established himself as one of the most accomplished illustrative painters of his time, whether the subject was a Border ballad, an incident in the life of Christ or, as here, a key moment in the religious history of Europe.

83. (above left) **Amelia Hill**, *David Octavius Hill*, 1868. Amelia Hill was the sister of Joseph Noel Paton and wife of David Octavius Hill. She was among the first women to be able to make a successful career as an artist in Scotland. Among her works were major public commissions for statues of David Livingstone (for Edinburgh) and Robert Burns (for Dumfries).

84. (above right) **William Fettes Douglas** *The Spell*, 1864. Like Joseph Noel Paton and James Drummond, Douglas was a fellow of the Society of Antiquaries of Scotland. Here he gives full expression to his antiquarian interest, evoking an earlier age of magic and alchemy.

the importance of this body should be stressed, for the portfolios of engravings it issued both provided income for artists and made their work available to a larger public. Paton was also notable for his interpretations of fairy scenes from Shakespeare, one of which received a prize at the Westminster Hall competitions in the 1840s, and for his response to Arthurian legend as reinterpreted by Tennyson. A friend of Paton who was also a regular illustrator of Arthurian legend at this time was James Archer (1823–1904), who is remembered today primarily for his Pre-Raphaelite influenced *Summer time in Gloucester* which is of particular interest for its fluid handling of the landscape background. Where Drummond and Paton emphasised the antiquarian object, William Fettes Douglas added a fascination with antiquarian books and what could be found in them. In *The Spell* (1864) he shows a magician with a shelf of thick volumes about to invoke the dead; a perhaps intentional gloss on the antiquarian process which so preoccupied him. Douglas was a contemporary of the poet, novelist and mystic George Macdonald (1824–1905) whose novel *Phantases* was published in 1858. He was also a significant painter of landscape, as was Joseph Noel Paton's brother, Waller Hugh Paton (1828–95) who produced some highly interesting work of concentrated detail influenced by Ruskin's ideas; indeed he may well have

84

attended Ruskin's Edinburgh lectures of 1853. Other landscape painters of the time included Arthur Perigal (1816–84), Alexander Fraser (1827–99), son of Wilkie's colleague of the same name, and Carlisle-born Sam Bough (1822–78) whose works around St Andrews and Dundee are of particular note.

Another talented Paton sibling was the sculptor Amelia Hill (1820–1904), who married David Octavius Hill but is remembered as a leading artist in her own right. This was no mean achievement for, as will be obvious to the reader, up to this date women had played only a small role in Scottish art. Had society allowed, women such as Anne Forbes (1745–1834), Margaret Adam (d. 1820), the Nasmyth sisters Elizabeth (1793–1862), Anne (1798–1874) and Charlotte (1804–84), and many others would have been able to take their rightful place as artists. As it is, Amelia Hill has to be considered as Scotland's first major woman artist of the modern period. The work of her contemporary, the painter Jemima Blackburn (1823–1909) should also be noted.

Robert Scott Lauder and his Students
The period of the painting of history, religion and legend which had begun with the work of Hamilton and Runciman reached both its zenith and a radical turning point in the work of a group of

83

painters a decade or two younger than Paton and Douglas. These were the pupils of Robert Scott Lauder. Lauder's brilliance as a teacher, in his role as Master of the Trustees' Academy from 1852 to 1861, tends to obscure his own contribution as a painter. Like D. O. Hill he had been a pupil of Andrew Wilson at the Trustees' Academy and subsequently studied in London, making particular use of the collection of the British Museum to hone his skills as a draughtsman. He travelled to Rome in the 1830s and on his return worked for over a decade in London before returning to Edinburgh as Master of the Trustees' Academy. Lauder's already mentioned *Christ Teacheth Humility* displays both his knowledge of old masters and his own originality. It is one of a number of works devoted to biblical scenes. That he was also a portrait painter of distinction can be seen in his *David Roberts in Oriental Dress* (1840) and another engaging work is his double portrait, *John Gibson Lockhart and his wife Charlotte Sophia Scott* (c. 1840). The latter shows Sir Walter Scott's son-in-law and daughter and it is a touching memorial to a loving relationship, for while Lockhart's portrait is taken from life, the image of his wife is posthumous for she had died in 1837. Robert Scott Lauder's achievement as a teacher was to create a school of painting in which the stylistic and conceptual diversity of his students was encouraged. But at the same time this diversity was grounded in a common mastery of drawing the figure both from casts and from the nude, together with a high competence in portraiture. Like many great teachers he was regarded as too experimental by some of his fellows, not least the new generation led by Paton, Drummond and Archer, who submitted a report critical of Lauder's methods to the Royal Scottish Academy in 1858. The next year the Academy established a conservatively taught life class in which Lauder had no part. In 1861 Lauder had a stroke which prevented him painting and this marks the effective end of the Trustees' Academy as a teaching institution of real importance.

All the notable painters who began their careers in the 1850s and 1860s were taught or influenced by Robert Scott Lauder. They include Robert Herdman (1828–88), William Quiller Orchardson (1832–1910), George Paul Chalmers (1833–78), William McTaggart (1835–1910), Hugh Cameron (1835–1918), Peter Graham (1836–1921), John MacWhirter (1839–1911), John Pettie (1839–93), Thomas Graham (1840–1906) and the Burr brothers, John (1831–93) and Alexander (1835–99). He also taught the sculptor John Hutchison (1833–1910). Within this group one finds a range of activity which extends from Scottish

85

85. **Robert Scott Lauder** *John Gibson Lockhart and his wife Charlotte Sophia Scott,* c. 1840. A touching work which shows the sensitivity of which Lauder was capable as a portraitist: the portrait of Lockhart is from life, that of his wife, Sir Walter Scott's daughter, Sophia, is posthumous.

86. **John Pettie** *Disbanded*,
1877. Like his teacher, Lauder,
John Pettie was well-known for
his paintings of events from
Scottish history, often related to
the works of Sir Walter Scott. Here
he shows a disbanded Jacobite
Highlander, complete with looted
Hanoverian equipment in his
knapsack. Note the freedom of
his use of paint which contrasts
markedly with the high finish
favoured by Joseph Noel Paton.

history painting to the stirrings of Modernism. The type of painting of historical events and related fictional scenes had been developed by William Allan and Robert Scott Lauder himself, and was taken on in particular by Robert Herdman. At the other end of the continuum a radical exploration of the relationship of paint, texture and colour to land, sea and community can be found in the work of William McTaggart. Yet early work by McTaggart can be very similar to early work by Herdman, reflecting Lauder's strong influence on both. Between these two poles fall the drawing room dramas and history paintings of Orchardson and Pettie, and the

87. **Peter Graham** *Wandering Shadows*, 1878. Another of Lauder's students, Peter Graham built on the by then well-established appetite for Scottish mountain and moorland landscapes, providing a backdrop in the imagination for the dramatic figures of Pettie.

post-McCulloch landscape spectacles of Peter Graham and John MacWhirter. Like Thomas Faed a decade earlier, Orchardson, Pettie, MacWhirter, Peter Graham and Thomas Graham settled in London in the 1860s and Hugh Cameron followed in the 1870s. By this time the energy of the early Pre-Raphaelite period was dissipating. The work of these artists in London reflects an aesthetically uncritical situation. Orchardson's and Pettie's anecdotes of European and Scottish history and the domestic life of the aristocracy raised few difficult questions in the mind of the viewer. Similarly the expansive landscapes of Peter Graham and John

86

88

87

88. **William Quiller Orchardson**
Voltaire, 1883. Orchardson's
engaging interpretations of history
are given power as images by his
inventive exploration of the picture
space and innovative use of paint.

MacWhirter served to underpin the developing stereotype of
Scotland as a land of the mountain and the flood, as Sir Walter
Scott so memorably put it. On the other hand MacWhirter's
observational ability and skill as a painter of nature had led Ruskin
to use his drawings of Norwegian wild-flowers to illustrate
lectures, while Thomas Graham's *Alone in London* is both a post-
Dickensian icon of potential urban hardship and an evocative
symbol of the Celt abroad. It should also be remembered that, as
one would expect of pupils of Lauder, these were technically
experimental artists; for example Orchardson's method of building up an image from small, linear brushstrokes and his theatrical

understanding of the picture space deserve recognition. In addition his art was brilliantly illustrative, engravings of works such as *Napoleon on board the Bellerophon* (1880) taking their place in many a home and schoolroom. As well as painting historical anecdote and scenes from Scott's novels, Pettie had a deserved reputation as a portrait painter and he exemplifies the fact that these London-Scottish artists, though hardly radical, were nevertheless highly interesting figures who reflected and contributed to their time and place. Of those who stayed in Edinburgh Robert Herdman produced works of vivid illustrative quality which owe something to the example of Thomas Faed as well as to Robert Scott Lauder. Among these are *Mary Queen of Scots' Farewell to*

89. (above right) **George Paul Chalmers** *The Legend*, 1864–78. This shows the continuing importance of Wilkie to artists fifty years his junior, and at the same time reflects a strong interest in the artists of the Hague school.

90. (right) **Robert Herdman** *After the Battle: A Scene in Covenanting Times*, 1870. Herdman's depiction of scenes from Scottish history range from Covenanter struggle to the deeds of St Columba.

91. **Hugh Cameron** *A Lonely Life*, 1873. As with Chalmers, Cameron's debt to contemporary Dutch artists is considerable and can be seen in this work.

France (1867) and *After the Battle: A Scene in Covenanting Times*   90
(1870). By contrast Chalmers and Cameron had begun to explore   89
a language of genre which owed a direct debt to Wilkie, and a   91
language of landscape which indicates a keen awareness of contemporary Netherlandish and French painting. These are often
paintings of low tones and subdued colour informed by a silvery,
northern light. Such an approach can be seen also in the landscapes of the Aberdonian George Reid (1841–1913), an occasional
student at the Trustees' Academy, who was certainly influenced
and probably taught by Lauder. Reid became a successful portrait
painter and was in due course elected president of the Royal
Scottish Academy but he is at his best in these early landscapes   92
which unite insights from the Hague and Barbizon Schools.
Reid was able to see examples of the work of these schools in
the collection of John Forbes White in Aberdeen and White
also enabled Reid to study in Netherlands. Along with that

of Chalmers, Cameron and McTaggart, Reid's work acted as an impulse to the next generation of Scottish painters.

The work produced by the artists taught by Lauder made possible the establishment of remarkable collections, among them that of James Guthrie Orchar (1825–98) of Dundee. Orchar was one of the most interesting patrons of this period for his business acumen was matched by an aesthetic sensibility. He had made his fortune supplying new machinery to the textile mills in Dundee and his own personal collection and his influence on the acquisitions policy of the city show that he was very conscious of the significance of Robert Scott Lauder and his students. Orchar was a close friend of Lauder's outstanding student William McTaggart, who was the herald of modern art in Scotland.

Born in 1835, McTaggart matches Wilkie's importance as an individual presence in Scottish art. He can be thought of as part of a European avant-garde, yet paradoxically he rarely left Scotland. Like his fellows he was impressed early on, apart from Lauder's teaching, by the Hague School, not least Joseph Israels. He had also seen work by Millais and Holman Hunt in Manchester in 1857 and he would have been aware of the Perth setting of Millais' *Autumn Leaves*, with the unmistakable outline of Ben Vorlich and Stuc a' Chroin on the skyline. The specificity of this landscape reference would have intrigued McTaggart, for his entire career can be seen as an attempt to bring figure and landscape into a conjunction both moral and optical. In early works he draws on the example of George Harvey one of whose illustrations to Burns' *Auld Lang Syne*, made for a portfolio published by the Royal Association for the Promotion of the Fine Arts in Scotland, bears a compositional relationship to McTaggart's painting *Spring* (1864). In this picture McTaggart breaks through his student Pre-Raphaelitism to show the beginnings of the freedom of oil-painting technique which was to characterize his later work. Whether there was any direct influence of French Impressionism on McTaggart is a matter of debate, although just as the Impressionists owed something to Constable, so also did McTaggart; indeed Leslie's *Memoir of the Life of John Constable* was among his most valued books. The differences between McTaggart's project and that of the Impressionists was that, whatever his interest in the effects of light and the texture of paint, McTaggart was at heart a social realist. He came from a Gaelic-speaking fishing and crofting family in Kintyre, so when he painted a coastal scene he understood what he was painting from a socially engaged perspective. What interested McTaggart was not so much the quasi-scientific

92. **George Reid** *Evening*, 1873.
Reid benefited from the patronage
of John Forbes White in Aberdeen,
and from close links with Lauder's
students in Edinburgh.

93. (opposite) **William McTaggart**
The Sailing of the Emigrant Ship,
1895. Perhaps the greatest of
McTaggart's visual explorations
of Scottish society and history.
The tragedy and hope of
emigration are given immediacy
by the artist's memory of events
in the west Highlands during his
own childhood.

interpretation of the effects of light which so concerned Monet
(1840–1926) as the conveying of the nature of a real place, with
real people and real history. Stylistically his work may have more
in common with that of the French painter but in the direction of
his thinking he is perhaps closer to Winslow Homer (1836–1901)
or indeed to the early interests of his younger contemporary, Vincent van Gogh (1853–90). In *The Storm*, from 1890, Frontis
McTaggart creates a spectacular image, but inherent to it is an
understanding of the consequences of bad weather for a coastal
community of men, women and children. A painter of a later generation, J. D. Fergusson, wrote that he could not imagine that
anyone had painted the sea better than McTaggart. This achievement comes into focus when one reflects that for McTaggart
the sea was not just an occasion for optical effects, it was the source
of life and death in his community of origin. McTaggart thus
integrated his Highland background into his work, making no
distinction between his modern self as an artist and the traditions
of his folk. This comes out powerfully in *The Coming of St Columba* 94
(1895), which shows Columba arriving in Kintyre in the sixth
century, prior to his settlement in Iona. It is a timeless image of a
Celtic space which is both ancient and modern.

McTaggart's engagement with his subject matter is at its height in a series of paintings in which he draws directly on his own youthful memories of the Highland Clearances. This is the series of 'Emigrant Ship' paintings, which includes *The Sailing of the Emigrant Ship* (1895), a masterpiece by any standard. Lindsay Errington notes that the 'composition was never intended as a news style record of any one emigrant group's departure', but was rather 'an emotionally charged reflection or recollection of Scottish Highland emigration as a whole'. She quotes one critic of 1899 who wrote that 'it is the epic of depopulation and emigration'. A remarkable aspect of these paintings is that they reflect on a crisis in Highland culture in a way wholly linked to McTaggart's reflection of the early years of the Gaels in Scotland, as symbolized by the coming of Columba. *The Emigrant Ship* series thus complements his 'Columba' paintings as part of a deeply felt personal

93

94. **William McTaggart** *The Coming of St Columba*, 1895. Depicting an event symbolic of the establishment of Christianity in the west of Scotland in the sixth century, McTaggart gives the coming of Columba to Kintyre an entirely modern treatment. Taken along with his emigrant ship paintings, this can be seen as part of a visual exploration of Highland history.

commentary on the history of the Gael. John Stuart Blackie, Professor of Greek at the University of Edinburgh, was an advocate of the Celtic Revival of which these works by McTaggart can be considered part. Summing up the problems of land use in the Highlands, Blackie wrote that 'the economical capacities of the Highlands are not to be understood by a few idle young gentlemen from the metropolis, who travel over the bare brown moors for ten days or a fortnight in the autumn, and then conceit themselves that they have seen the country'. It is ironic to reflect that such young gentlemen on their return home to London or Edinburgh would be likely to see the Highlands as no more than a post-Landseer spectacle through the eyes of artists such as Peter Graham, McTaggart's fellow student at the Trustees' Academy. What McTaggart had done was to offer an alternative to that view

both moral and technical. Some protection for those living in the Highlands was afforded by the passing of the Crofters' Holdings Act in 1886, and this illustrates the current nature of the issues that McTaggart addressed.

Heroes and Monuments

Although McTaggart's *Columba* paintings are among the least heroic in style that one can imagine, they are nevertheless part of the nineteenth-century trend to represent national figures of heroic status. Indeed, at around the same time McTaggart was painting these works there was a proposal from Patrick Geddes for a large statue of St Columba at the head of the Lawnmarket in Edinburgh. From the 1830s onwards there had been a strong growth in such sculptural representations. These were not only of Scottish figures but also of British figures relevant to Scotland such as the Duke of Wellington, whose massive bronze equestrian monument by John Steell (1804–91) outside Register House in Edinburgh attracted large crowds to its opening in 1856. Samuel Joseph, Thomas Campbell and Lawrence Macdonald had created the conditions for the success of this next generation of Scottish sculptors which included, as well as Steell, Patrick Park (1811–55), Alexander Handyside Ritchie (1804–1870) and William Calder Marshall (1813–94). John Steell was the first Scottish sculptor to have a real impact on the making of public sculpture in Scotland. Although half a century younger than Raeburn his career has a real analogy with that of the painter for they both demonstrated that patronage within Scotland itself was sufficient to sustain their respective media at a high level. Steell's father had a keen interest in art for he was the owner of a wood carving business which carried out a number of major architectural commissions including work for the Signet Library in Edinburgh. The young John thus had relevant experience from an early age. He was educated at the Trustees' Academy and in Rome. That he became a full member of the Scottish Academy in 1830 while still in his twenties is an indication of the high regard in which his contemporaries held him. Two years later he made his public mark with the exhibition of his *Alexander and Bucephalus*. In 1838 his design for a memorial to Sir Walter Scott was exhibited to great acclaim. Although as a sculpture it was not eligible for the architectural competition for a monument to the author, it was adopted as the central element of the Gothic spire designed by George Meikle Kemp and is now an integral part of that edifice on Princes Street in Edinburgh. Such work marks the coming to maturity of a national school of

95

sculpture, which had as its focus a reinterpretation of Scottish cultural history through the writings of Burns and Scott and the moral preoccupations of preachers such as Thomas Chalmers. Some years before there had been a significant architectural manifestation of this cultural nationalism in the form of the Jacobite monument at Glenfinnan, designed in 1815 by an early supporter of John Steell, the architect James Gillespie Graham (1776–1855). In 1834 the figure of a Highlander by John Greenshields (1795–1835) was added to the top of the tower.

Younger contemporaries of Steell who contributed to this project of historical self-consciousness were William Brodie (1815–81) and Amelia Hill (1820–1904), and one of the sculptors who took it forward in the next generation was John Steell's student David Watson Stevenson (1842–1904). Perhaps the most fascinating of all Stevenson's work is his statue of William Wallace (1887), 96 sword aloft, which completes the exterior of the National Wallace Monument built on Abbey Craig near Stirling in 1869. It overlooks the site of Wallace's victory over the forces of Edward I of England at Stirling Bridge in 1297. Yet as in the sixteenth

95. **John Steell** *Sir Walter Scott*, 1840–46. This work, the main sculptural element of the Scott Monument in Edinburgh, helped to establish Steell as the first Scottish sculptor of the modern period to make a successful career in Scotland itself. He gave energy and direction to a school of heroic sculpture which found its zenith in the multitude of statues made for the exterior of the Scottish National Portrait Gallery in the 1890s.

96. **David Watson Stevenson**
William Wallace, 1887. A pupil of John Steell, Stevenson created some of the most memorable Scottish heroic sculpture in the second half of the nineteenth century, including this image of William Wallace for the exterior of the National Wallace Monument near Stirling.

century the most radical plastic expression is in the architecture of which this sculpture is a part, the tower by J. T. Rochead (1814–78), which is a Scots-Baronial cross between a cathedral and a castle. While the outside of the monument carries a figure of Wallace, inside is a gallery of heroes. It contains portrait busts (again mostly by Stevenson) of, among others, Robert the Bruce, Robert Burns, Sir Walter Scott, Adam Smith, Thomas Chalmers, David Livingstone, Hugh Miller, George Buchanan, John Knox, James Watt, David Brewster and Thomas Carlyle. Taken as an architectural and sculptural whole, the monument is a stunning example of northern European National Romanticism, in which cultural identity is composed in equal parts of heroism in battle, poetry, piety, economic theory and practical science. The latter area is emphasized by the inclusion not only of James Watt but also of his younger colleague William Murdoch, the inventor of gas lighting. The literary context of this monument should also be noted. As Elspeth King has pointed out, in the years prior to the building of the National Wallace Monument one of the most

common books in Scottish households, along with the Bible and Burns, was William Hamilton of Gilbertfield's modernized edition (1772) of Blind Harry's *Wallace*, a poem originally composed in the late fifteenth century. D. W. Stevenson's younger contemporary, T. S. Burnett (1853–88), made further sculptures which contributed to the heroic vein, for example his *Rob Roy* (1883).

Public sculpture gained a particular boost in 1896 with the centenary of the death of Robert Burns, which led to numerous commissions. Just as Goethe's comments on James Macpherson are of interest, so too are his views on Burns. He admired Burns greatly and was convinced that Burns's songs would endure and, as he put it, 'greet us from the mouths of the people'. This was a prescient view of the enthusiasm that would be expressed in the centenary celebrations. D. W. Stevenson was at the forefront with commissions for a figure of Burns in Leith and his *Highland Mary* at Dunoon. The interest in Burns statues (and also those of Scott) was extensive throughout the English-speaking, Scottish-settled world. John Steell himself had been commissioned to produce a figure in bronze for Central Park in New York, unveiled in 1880. Versions of this were made for Dundee, London and Dunedin. Such works were very popular, crowds of many thousands attending their unveilings. Multiple versions of Burns statues were not unusual; for example the London sculptor F. W. Pomeroy (1856–1924) made a notable image of the poet as ploughman, casts of which can be found in Paisley, Sydney and Auckland. Amelia Hill made a statue for Dumfries and Pittendrigh Macgillivray

97. (opposite) **Pittendrigh Macgillivray** *Robert Burns*, 1895. In this maquette for his Burns statue in Irvine, Macgillivray (himself a poet as well as an artist) gave one of the finest sculptural accounts of Burns.

98. (below) **William Hole** *Processional Frieze* (detail), 1898–1901. This final portion of the frieze from the entrance hall of the Scottish National Portrait Gallery shows, among others, David Wilkie and David Livingstone. In total the frieze comprises over one hundred and fifty figures. It ends with the image of Thomas Carlyle, whose essays *On Heroes, Hero-worship and the Heroic in History* had been influential on the projects for portrait galleries in both London and in Edinburgh.

(1856–1938), a fine poet himself, made a vigorous figure of Burns for Irvine. Such sculptural celebrations were paralleled in painting and graphic work. David Allan, Alexander Nasmyth, David Wilkie and D. O. Hill have already been mentioned, but among many other examples one might add William Bell Scott's illustrations from the 1830s and John Faed's paintings made for engraving in the 1850s. This interest in Burns has continued up to the time of writing in the work of a number of artists including George Wyllie (b. 1921) and Lys Hansen (b. 1935).

If one takes the building of early monuments to Burns in the first decades of the nineteenth century as the beginning of the period of intense advocacy of Scottish heroes, the trend can be considered to reach its height in the establishment of the Scottish National Portrait Gallery. This was designed by Robert Rowand Anderson (1834–1921) and opened in 1889. It is not just a portrait gallery; it is an architectural expression of its purpose as a portrait gallery, an unlikely reflection of Louis Sullivan's contemporary dictum 'form follows function'. The exterior surface has numerous statues of figures from Scottish history many of which were carried out either by the most innovative sculptor of the day Pittendrigh Macgillivray or by William Birnie Rhind (1853–1933). Other sculptors involved included the latter's brother John Rhind (1858–1936), John Hutchison, D. W. Stevenson, his brother William Grant Stevenson (1849–1919), Archibald McFarlane Shannan (1850–1915) and Waller Hubert Paton (*fl.* 1881–1932), son of the painter Waller Hugh Paton. The equivocation with which even the most Presbyterian of artistically minded Scots have always regarded John Knox was reflected in the fact that the cost of most of the statues was met by public subscription – but not that of Knox. The memory of the sermon 'Against Idolatry' and its destructive consequences for the art of Scotland dies hard. In the entrance hall the exterior sculptural scheme was echoed and enhanced by murals including a remarkable frieze on a gilded background depicting a procession of about one hundred and fifty separate figures extending back from Thomas Carlyle to the Stone Age. Carlyle is a particularly appropriate anchor here, for his 1840 lectures *Heroes, Hero-worship and the Heroic in History* had helped to shape the notion of this gallery and its London counterpart in the first place. On the walls of the balcony above the frieze are large panels on subjects such as *The Mission of Columba* and *The Battle of Largs*. The frieze and the panels are the work of William Hole (1846–1917), an artist who contributed greatly to the illustrative tradition.

Chapter 7: Modernity and Revivals

The Glasgow School of Painting

In the 1880s the artistic leadership of Scotland passed decisively to young artists associated with Glasgow. The 1870s and 1880s were times of great expansion of exhibiting, the Royal Scottish Academy on occasion showing over a thousand works in its annual exhibition. However, the success of the Academy was an Edinburgh success and it was difficult for artists who had not set up their studios in the capital to make an impression. One reaction to this was the establishment of the Glasgow Institute as an exhibiting body in 1861, an initiative complemented by the patronage available as a result of Glasgow's growing commercial and industrial strength. It is symbolic of this westwards shift that the most

99. **John Lavery** *The Tennis Party*, 1885. Studying in France was fundamental to the achievement of the Glasgow school of painters. In this image of the Glasgow bourgeoisie at play, John Lavery paints in a manner that, as well as displaying his own willingness to experiment with composition, shows a keen awareness of the work of both Bastien-Lepage and Degas.

innovative paintings being made in the 1880s by Edinburgh-based artists were those of artists with their origins in the west, namely William McTaggart and a painter strongly influenced by him, James Lawton Wingate (1846–1924). The passive state of the Academy led, eventually, to the setting up in Edinburgh in 1891 of the more radically inclined Society of Scottish Artists. But in the late 1870s the most promising young painter from the east of the country, Arthur Melville (1855–1904), shared a vision of what painting could be with like-minded counterparts in Glasgow. Although Melville remained distinct from it, he is often considered along with this Glasgow School. These artists were to dominate the 1880s with an intimate approach to landscape and portraiture which owed much to the Hague and Barbizon schools on the one hand and to Whistler on the other. Those at the heart of this Glasgow School – often referred to as the 'Glasgow Boys' – were Robert Macaulay Stevenson (1854–1952), James Paterson (1854–1932), William York Macgregor (1855–1923), John Lavery (1856–1941), George Henry (1858–1943), James Guthrie (1859–1930), William Kennedy (1859–1918), Edward Arthur Walton (1860–1922),

Joseph Crawhall (1861–1913), Alexander Roche (1861–1921), and Edward Atkinson Hornel (1864–1933). The sculptor Pittendrigh Macgillivray was also associated with the group and on its periphery were painters such as David Gauld (1865–1936), Stuart Park (1862–1933) and also older artists such as James Elder Christie (1847–1914) and Thomas Millie Dow (1848–1919). One must also mention the talented but short-lived Bessie MacNicol (1869–1904), who, although she was a few years younger than the others, makes clear the limitation of the term 'Glasgow Boys'. An innovative contemporary whose life and work remained relatively distinct was the Paisley watchmaker John Quinton Pringle (1864–1925). Also of interest here is James McLachlan Nairn (1859–1904) who was very much part of the Glasgow School before leaving for Dunedin in 1890. Subsequently, along with the Dutch painter Petrus van der Velden (1836–1913), he helped to establish painting in New Zealand. In a complementary role to the Glasgow School artists was Alexander Reid (1854–1924), one of the most perceptive dealers in European art of his day. Reid shared accommodation in Paris with Vincent and Theo van Gogh, and Vincent painted a fine portrait of him in 1886. Reid was both a source of information for the Glasgow Boys about developments on the Continent and an advocate and supporter of their work.

What united the Glasgow School as artists was a distrust of the mountain and moorland spectacles that had been pioneered by Horatio McCulloch, developed by Peter Graham and John MacWhirter and made routine by numerous imitators content to paint heather and hill and Highland cattle. By contrast these painters looked to France, the new centre of gravity of European art. At this time Glasgow collectors were showing considerable interest not only in the Hague School but also in the artists of Barbizon, indeed they were at the forefront of collecting in Britain in this respect. Other important influences came from south of the Border, not least through the experience of William York Macgregor as a student of Alphonse Legros at the Slade. Macgregor was among the eldest of the Glasgow Boys and had an informal leadership role, for classes held in his studio were a key meeting point. But while Macgregor was educated at the Slade, Walton studied in Dusseldorf and then at Glasgow School of Art, where he met Guthrie who subsequently studied with Pettie in London. Hornel studied first at the Trustees' Academy in Edinburgh (by then almost defunct), and then at Antwerp, while Alexander Roche went to a few classes at Glasgow School of Art and then to Paris where he studied under, among others, Gérôme. The group is thus notable for its interplay of differing educational influences of which the two most common are study in Glasgow and in Paris. James Paterson, for example, was almost wholly Paris-educated, while George Henry studied in Glasgow, both at the School of Art and with Macgregor. Arthur Melville studied at the Royal Scottish Academy Schools in Edinburgh and subsequently visited Paris. John Lavery studied in Glasgow and London and then at the Académie Julian and the Atelier Colarossi in Paris. On the other hand Crawhall's education was almost informal. Another influence was McTaggart, although it can be noted that many of McTaggart's finest works were made in the 1880s and 1890s and are thus contemporary with Glasgow School activity. In addition the concern of these painters with exploration of balanced tonal values across a relatively constricted scene contrasted markedly with McTaggart's emphasis on the sea and the horizon, although their concerns do relate to village and farm scenes by McTaggart, and to similar subjects by Chalmers and Cameron.

Again reflecting the French influence and that of McTaggart, the Glasgow School was the first group of Scottish painters to be committed to painting in the open air. The effect of this was predictable but profound. The artistic geography of Scotland changed as it was explored by painters not for romantic backdrops to be sketched and then finished in the studio, but for places in which it was possible to settle down and observe during the summer months. In the late 1870s and early 1880s Paterson and Macgregor favoured the east coast around Fife and Kincardineshire, while Walton, Crawhall and Guthrie preferred the Roseneath peninsular in the Firth of Clyde and subsequently – along with George Henry – Brig o'Turk in the Trossachs. In due course Cockburnspath in East Lothian, Moniaive in Dumfriesshire, and Kirkcudbright were also favoured places. Outside Scotland Lavery, Kennedy and Roche made their base from 1883 in the French village Grez-sur-Loing, near Fontainebleau, where they joined an international community of artists, many of whom were influenced by Jules Bastien-Lepage. Active there were kindred spirits such as William Stott of Oldham and the Irishman Frank O'Meara. The importance of Grez in the development of Lavery's work in particular is hard to overestimate. He derived much from Stott and O'Meara, indeed the latter became a close friend. Lavery's paintings of rowers on the river and figures on the bank around the bridge at Grez are subtle essays in backlighting, reflected light and muted sunlight. The originality of these works lies also in Lavery's interest in the figure in active movement and he developed this back in

100. William York Macgregor
The Vegetable Stall, 1883–84.
With this painting Macgregor set
a standard of engaged objectivity
perhaps not seen again until the
seascapes of Joan Eardley three
quarters of a century later.

101. (opposite) **James
Guthrie** *A Hind's Daughter*,
1883. Direct in composition,
in subject and in technique,
Guthrie creates an image of
rural life which, despite shared
influences, contrasts markedly
with the paintings of gentler
pastimes so favoured by Lavery.

Scotland in *The Tennis Party* (1885). Although the group thus split into French-based and Scottish-based wings, the inspiration of Corot, Millet and in particular of Bastien-Lepage was felt equally by all. These shared influences did not lead to a lessening of individuality. For example, although both Lavery and Guthrie owe much to Bastien-Lepage, Lavery's gently recreational bourgeois idylls contrast markedly with Guthrie's uncompromising representation of rural life and work. The latter's *A Hind's Daughter* (1883) builds in its immediacy on his *Highland Funeral* finished the year before. *A Hind's Daughter* is a remarkable example of the absorption of French influence and its transformation in a Scottish context. It is a straightforward and unsentimental work – much more so indeed than was typical of Bastien-Lepage – which develops a direct language of oil paint in which marks of brush and palette knife are evident, a style which was echoed in Macgregor's *Vegetable Stall* painted a year later. These works are as far as possible removed from the smooth finish of earlier but still living painters such as Joseph Noel Paton. Guthrie and Macgregor were concerned with the objective nature of both subject and medium. One of the consequences of this sort of approach throughout Europe was a growth in regard for the painting as an object in its own right, rather than simply a representation of a scene or an

idea, and the stylistic ruggedness of these painters contributes to
this. Such features can be seen also in Walton's *A Berwickshire* 102
Fieldworker (1884). Attention to the nature of paint also led to a
consideration of decorative qualities and Glasgow School work
was acclaimed for its 'decorative harmony' when it was exhibited
in Munich in 1890. Such harmony can be seen in Arthur Melville's
early works such as *Audrey and her Goats* (1884–89). The painting,
which takes its subject from *As You Like It*, is a statement about
nature, literature and art worthy of Ruskin, for Audrey is the least
'artful' and most 'natural' of all Shakespeare's characters. The
decorative trend was carried further in the work of George Henry
and E. A. Hornel. They combined a lightening of palette with an
increased emphasis on what has been described by Hornel's biographer Bill Smith as 'abstracted colour rather than observed colour'.
Here the example of the French painter Adolphe Monticelli
(1824–86) was important. Monticelli was popular in Glasgow and
of great interest to dealers like Reid. His works foreshadow the

almost tapestry-like effect of paint that Henry and Hornel developed although Monticelli has little in common with the sheer energy of composition found in works by Hornel from 1891, such as *The Brook* and *Summer*. Compositionally these owe much to Japanese prints and the same is true of George Henry's important *Galloway Landscape* (1889), which unifies a direct approach to landforms with a consciousness of the decorative possibilities of two-dimensional form. This approach resonates with Paul Gauguin's contemporary explorations of Breton and West Indian landscape and also with the formal language that Edvard Munch was developing in Norway. Both David Gauld and Bessie MacNicol were influenced by the decorative approach of Hornel and Henry but both developed their own directions. Gauld utilized flat areas of textured colour with compositional links to stained glass (which he also designed) and MacNicol became a painter in whose work emphasis on the figure is combined with a keen sense of composition and decorative values. Works such as *A French Girl* (1895), *A Girl of the 'Sixties'* (1899) and *Vanity* (1902), leave one conscious of a considerable talent never fully expressed. MacNicol's death in childbirth at the age of thirty-four is thus all the more the more poignant. In watercolours such as *Mediterranean Port* (1892), Arthur Melville extended the formal explorations of the Glasgow School into a world of pure colour in which landscape, although completely identifiable, is subordinated to the experience of intensity of hue.

105

103

104

103. **Bessie MacNicol** *A Girl of the 'Sixties'*, 1899. Several years younger than others of the Glasgow school, Bessie MacNicol was a highly talented painter whose style was influenced by her friendship with E. A. Hornel and George Henry. Her death at the age of thirty-five cut short a promising career.

Extensive trips to the European and North African coasts of the Mediterranean were fundamental and Melville brought this radical colourism united with his highly successful 'blottesque' watercolour technique back to Scotland. That technique was taken up by the talented watercolour painter James Watterston Herald (1859–1914). Along with the experiments of Hornel and Henry, Melville's works were to have a lasting effect on the attitude of Scottish painters to the use of colour.

The work of the London-based American painter James Abbott McNeill Whistler (1835–1903) was a subtle and continuing presence for the Glasgow School, and it was largely through Walton's efforts that Whistler's *Carlyle* (1872–73) was acquired for the municipal collection of Glasgow in 1891. Whistler had helped to transmit an enthusiasm for Japanese culture to Britain and Henry and Hornel took this further for they visited Japan itself, leaving early in 1893 and returning a year and a half later. This journey was made possible by financial support from Alexander Reid and the collector William Burrell and a number of notable works resulted, including Hornel's *Kite Flying, Japan* (1894) and Henry's *Japanese Lady with a Fan* (1894). The wider Japanese influence in Scotland was to be felt in due course in the designs of Charles Rennie Mackintosh and his colleagues. It was also present in the

104. **Arthur Melville**
Mediterranean Port, 1892. Although he had little connection with Glasgow, Melville shared many of the concerns of the Glasgow school artists and he is often classed with them. He was one of the most innovative of all, making numerous trips to the Mediterranean to explore the effects of strong light and colour, as seen in this vivid watercolour.

107

105. (above) **George Henry**
A Galloway Landscape, 1889.
This work is a significant
contribution to the formal
reinterpetation of landscape in
the light of an awareness of the
conventions of Japanese wood-
block prints. Artists throughout
Europe, not least Gauguin, shared
this interest.

106. (right) **George Henry and
E. A. Hornel** *The Druids: Bringing
in the Mistletoe*, 1890. Not
constrained by their more usual
role as landscape painters, in this
joint work Hornel and Henry
made a seminal contribution to
the visual art of the Celtic Revival
in Scotland.

107. **Edward Atkinson Hornel**
Kite Flying, Japan, 1894.
Following up their interest in
Japanese art, Henry and Hornel
were among the few Western
artists of the period to visit
Japan itself. The result was an
intriguing attempt to synthesize
East and West.

linearity of illustration favoured by Celtic Revival artists in
Edinburgh; indeed one of Hornel's Japanese drawings appears
in 1895 in the magazine of that movement, *The Evergeen*. This
interaction of interests, the one exotic, the other historical is
characteristic of the time. Henry and Hornel had made a direct
contribution to Celtic Revival imagery with their collaborative
paintings *The Druids: Bringing in the Mistletoe* (1890) and *The Star*
in the East (1891). It should also be noted that John Lavery contributed to the Celtic Revival in Ireland. For the purposes of this
book Lavery is considered as very much part of the Scottish tradition but although he moved to Scotland as a young child he was

born in Belfast and from the early years of the twentieth century he had a second career as an Irish painter. Among a number of remarkable portraits are those of *Eamon de Valera* (1921) and a portrait in death of Michael Collins (1922). His most clearly Celtic Revival work is a portrait of his wife as *Kathleen ni Houlihan* (1927) which formed part of a design for a bank note. Lavery was by this time living in both Ireland and in London, where he was in demand as a society portrait painter. Other Glasgow School painters had also found a high-level of success. Walton, like Lavery, had established a reputation in London, as had Guthrie. The latter was appointed President of the Royal Scottish Academy from 1902 to 1919, and this indicates more than anything else the complete acceptance by the Scottish art world of the Glasgow School, although most of their more important works had been painted by about 1895.

Mackintosh's Glasgow

In the early 1890s a younger group of artists, designers and architects gathered round a fellow student at Glasgow School of Art, Charles Rennie Mackintosh (1868–1928). In 1891 James Guthrie himself had reckoned watercolours of Italian churches by Mackintosh the best of an exhibition of student work and had been distressed to hear that he was studying architecture. Although Mackintosh is primarily remembered as an architect, Guthrie's endorsement is a useful reminder of his outstanding ability as a painter. Guthrie's activities as a judge were not the only link between Mackintosh and the painters of the Glasgow School. David Gauld was a close friend and Bessie MacNicol studied at the School of Art at the same time, while E. A. Walton's brother, the designer George Walton (1868–1933), was a contemporary. All the more fascinating then is Mackintosh's distinctiveness as an artist. His imaginative symbolism is breathtaking in early water-colours such as *Harvest Moon* (1892). Working with him closely were his future wife Margaret Macdonald (1863–1933) and her sister Frances (1874–1921). Another co-worker was his fellow architecture student, Herbert MacNair (1868–1955), who was soon to marry Frances. This group, 'The Four', had a central role in the development of what became known as the Glasgow Style. The co-operative nature of this venture is manifest in images like the *Poster for The Glasgow Institute of the Fine Arts* (c. 1896), which at first glance one might think of as typical of Mackintosh but is in fact the work of Margaret Macdonald, Frances Macdonald and Herbert MacNair. Margaret Macdonald in particular has now

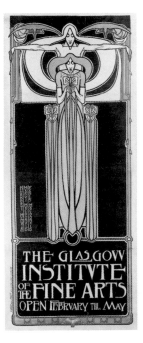

108. **Margaret Macdonald, Frances Macdonald and Herbert MacNair** *Poster for the Glasgow Institute of the Fine Arts*, c. 1896. At first sight a typical design by Charles Rennie Mackintosh, this poster is a reminder that the 'Mackintosh style' was in fact a joint project involving four artists. The other three, Herbert MacNair and the sisters Frances and Margaret Macdonald, are the designers of this work.

109

108

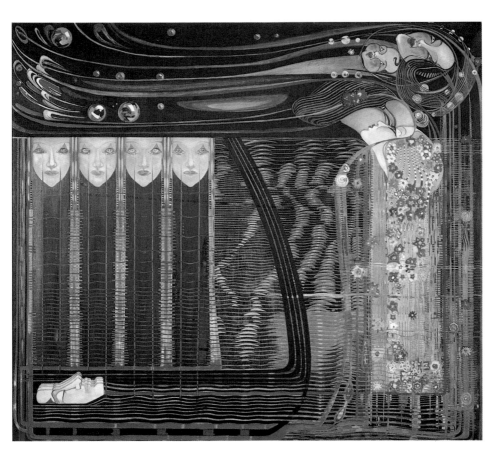

109. (opposite) **Charles Rennie Mackintosh** *Harvest Moon*, 1892. This watercolour of subtle and intriguing symbolism dates from Mackintosh's days as a student at Glasgow School of Art. It demonstrates that although best known as an architect, Mackintosh was an outstanding painter from the very beginning of his career.

110. (above) **Margaret Macdonald** *The Opera of the Sea*, c. 1916. Margaret Macdonald's achievement has tended to be overshadowed by that of her husband, Charles Rennie Mackintosh. Over recent years an increasing awareness of the quality of works such as this have enabled due regard to be given to her as an artist in her own right.

been given some of the individual credit she deserves as an artist for works such as the oil and tempera *Opera of the Sea* (c. 1916), originally designed as one of a pair of gesso panels in 1903. The Four opened the way for a wider group of Glasgow Style graphic and applied artists which included the illustrators Jessie M. King (1875–1949), Katherine Cameron (1874–1965) and Annie French (1872–1965), and the embroiderers Jessie Newbery (1864–1948), Ann MacBeth (1870–1948) and Muriel Boyd (1888–1981). Among other figures of interest were the painter Agnes Raeburn (1872–1955) and her sister Lucy (1869–1952), who edited the informal *Magazine* which brought together some of the most important early work by The Four. This blossoming of activity owes much to the Cornish painter Francis Newbery (1855–1946), who had been appointed as director of Glasgow School of Art in 1885, indeed the importance of his contribution as a teacher can be compared to that of Robert Scott Lauder. Part of his achievement

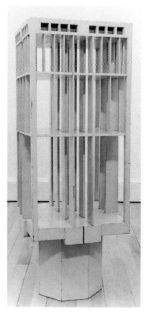

111. **Charles Rennie Mackintosh**
Revolving Bookcase for Hous'hill,
1904. Mackintosh's radical
treatment of three dimensional
design could hardly be better
represented than by this bookcase.
A symbolic tree of life is treated
with a minimalism worthy of the
International Style of the next
generation of European architects.

was to create a situation in which women were able to excel and in due course to take leadership roles. Several, including his wife Jessie, went on to head their respective areas at the School of Art.

The wider context for the development of the Glasgow Style was shipbuilding and engineering. This was not simply a question of a commercial climate that made money and patronage available. Nor was it simply a question of the School of Art catering for highly skilled practitioners of arts and crafts needed in the fitting out of ships. Above all it was a question of the aesthetics of marine architecture. These artists and designers had their childhood in the heyday of the Clyde-built tea clippers that are still a standard of beauty in ship design (the *Cutty Sark* was launched in 1869). As they became adults, elegant and technologically pioneering transatlantic liners such as the *City of New York* were being launched. Since Le Corbusier published *Towards an Architecture* in 1923 the inspirational effect of the transatlantic liner on the design of the 1920s has been taken for granted. The effect of living in the city at the heart of the world's shipbuilding industry should be given equal consideration with respect to the artists of the Glasgow Style a generation earlier. Direct artistic influences on the development of this style were diverse. Japan has been mentioned and the lectures and books of Glasgow-born Christopher Dresser were a further means of transmission of Japanese ideas. Although more inclined to formal experimentation, the artists of the Glasgow Style took as part of their conscious aesthetic foundation the ideas of the Arts and Crafts movement as put forward by William Morris and Walter Crane in the previous generation. Mackintosh in particular was influenced by the writings of the Arts and Crafts architect John Sedding, some of whose words he made into a personal motto: 'There is hope in honest error, none in the icy perfections of the mere stylist.' In 1901 these words were made by Mackintosh into an image which looks forward to the aesthetic of the Bauhaus a generation later. The influential London-based magazine *The Studio*, which had its roots in the Arts and Crafts movement, was an important source of contemporary visual thinking. It made available stylistic experimentations such as those of Aubrey Beardsley and, of particular importance to the Glasgow artists, Jan Toorop (1858–1928), the Dutch-Indonesian pioneer of the plant-inspired forms of Art Nouveau imagery. The Glasgow Style artists united these sinuous abstractions with their sensitivity to the exactness of proportion inherent in the practical geometrical tradition of Glasgow engineering. This unity can be seen in Mackintosh's 1904 design of the order desk chair for Miss

Cranston's Willow Tea Rooms in Sauchiehall Street. The form of this chair is based on the radically geometrized form of a willow tree. This work and others from the same period, such as the *Revolving Bookcase for Hous'hill*, bring to mind Ruskin's formal analysis of tree and leaf in *Modern Painters* and resonate with Mondrian's explorations of a few years later. The intense quality of this aspect of Mackintosh's work could not be clearer than in his structurally informed watercolours of flowers, which he made throughout his career. *The Studio* publicized the Glasgow Style as early as 1893, when the refurbished Glasgow Art Club, for which Mackintosh was mainly responsible, was reviewed, although Mackintosh himself was not named. In 1896 and 1897 the editor of *The Studio*, Gleeson White, wrote an influential three-part assessment entitled *Some Glasgow Designers*, beginning an advocacy that was to last twenty years, including the special publication, Jessie M. King's *Seven Happy Days* for Christmas, 1913.

111

112

A further influence was the Celtic Revival, which Thomas Howarth has called 'one of the most potent stimuli in the evolution of the Glasgow style'. Mackintosh's first executed design in stone, dating from 1888, was itself a link back to this Scottish past, a simple Celtic cross in memory of a colleague of his father. This grave marker took its place among many other Celtic crosses in the Glasgow Necropolis, all of which refer back in style to the high crosses of Iona and Islay of the eight and ninth centuries, or the later work of the West Highland School. The Necropolis also contains a fine gravestone in developed Glasgow Style from some twenty years later, designed by Mackintosh's friend Talwin Morris (1865–1911), who must also be mentioned. Morris had been closely involved with art magazine publishing in London and had come to Glasgow as art director with the publisher Blackie; it is members of the Blackie family that the gravestone commemorates. He was a designer of brilliance and produced book covers of characteristic Glasgow Style, uniting geometry with natural forms and Celtic Revival symbolism. It was through these mass-produced book covers that the Glasgow Style became familiar on an everyday level throughout the British Empire. Talwin Morris also played a key role in convincing Walter Blackie that Charles Rennie Mackintosh should be commissioned to design Blackie's new house overlooking the Clyde at Helensburgh. The result, Hill House (1902–4), has an importance in early twentieth-century domestic design which is perhaps only matched by Frank Lloyd Wright's Robie House (1909) in Chicago, and Adolf Loos' Steiner House (1910) in Vienna. One of the earliest to appreciate the merits of the Glasgow Style was the German cultural attaché Hermann Muthesius, who described Mackintosh in 1902 as one of the geniuses of modern architecture. Muthesius is now recognized as a major commentator on the development of twentieth-century design and through him there was substantial German interest in the Glasgow Style artists. Their work became well known in German-speaking countries through the magazines *Dekorative Kunst* and *Deutsche Kunst und Dekoration*; indeed the latter commissioned cover designs from both Jessie M. King and Margaret Macdonald in 1902. A strong link was forged with Austrian artists of the Vienna Secession, and The Four created a room for the 1900 Secession Exhibition which met with high acclaim and illuminated the shared domain of understanding between the Glasgow and Vienna artists. A key part of this shared understanding was that both groups had developed their pioneering modernism within a matrix of awareness of myth, legend and history.

Photography and Etching

We know the features of the artists of the Glasgow Style mainly through the work of the photographer James Craig Annan (1864–1946). His portraits include not only Mackintosh but Margaret Macdonald, Anna Muthesius (wife of Hermann), Jessie

113. **James Craig Annan**
Anna Muthesius, c. 1900.
James Craig Annan was a pioneer
of photogravure and it is in this
medium that we see his portrait
of Anna Muthesius, wife of the
German design theorist and
advocate of the Glasgow Style,
Hermann Muthesius.

M. King and Ann MacBeth. Annan was an equally fine photographer of landscape and in this regard he brings to mind the painting of the Glasgow School, for the inspiration of his photographs is the clarity of the Japanese print on the one hand and the rural vision of the Hague school on the other. Annan helped to mould the pictorialism of the Photo-Secession founded by his close contemporary Alfred Stieglitz (1864–1946) in New York in 1902. He contributed extensively to Stieglitz's journal, *Camera Work*, both in his own right and as advocate of the work of Hill and Adamson. One of the characteristics of this magazine was its use of photogravure as a means of reproduction. Both Annan and Stieglitz were interested in this process as a solution to the problem of the instability of the photographic image. Photogravure is a process of printing an ink image onto paper from an etched plate made from the photographic negative. This contrasts with the normal photographic process of printing the image directly from the negative onto light-sensitive paper. The attraction was that photogravure made the image permanent and in addition it could be manipulated in the same way as an etching. In this context, Annan's friendship with leading figures of the Scottish etching revival, including D. Y. Cameron (1865–1945) and William Strang (1859–1921), is of great inter- 115 est. The link is made clear in one of Annan's finest photogravure portraits, *The Etching Printer* (1902), which shows William Strang intently studying the fall of light on the surface of an inked etching plate. In Scotland the etching revival has its roots not only in Whistler's influence but also in an awareness of the pioneering work of John Clerk of Eldin and Alexander Runciman in the eighteenth century. Their skills had been transmitted to the mid-nineteenth century by Andrew Geddes, William Dyce and the brothers David and William Bell Scott. In due course etching was taken forward not only by Cameron and Strang but by Muirhead Bone (1876–1953), James McBey (1883–1959) and Ernest Lumsden (1883–1948). Each of these early twentieth-century printmakers was distinguished in a different way. McBey made images that show an extraordinary sensitivity to the potential for delicacy in the etched line. Lumsden went on to write what is still the standard book on etching, packed full of illuminating technical notes from individual artists. Muirhead Bone was renowned for his records of architecture and industry, for example his etching *The Great Gantry, Charing Cross* (1906). His expertise extended to lithography and this can be seen in *A Shipyard Scene* 114 *from a Big Crane* (1917), which again reminds one of the engineering context of the Glasgow Style.

114. Muirhead Bone *A Shipyard Scene from a Big Crane*, 1917. This startling lithograph with its viewpoint high above a Clyde shipyard, gives some idea of the vitality of the printmaking revival of which Muirhead Bone was part.

Both Cameron and Strang were sought after as painters as well as printmakers. Cameron was the elder brother of the illustrator Katherine Cameron but, despite studying at Glasgow School of Art and subsequently in Edinburgh, he remained distinct in his art from both the Glasgow Boys and his sister's Glasgow Style colleagues. Nevertheless, in the thoughtful simplifications of landscape and architecture which characterize both his etchings and oil paintings, he shares with both groups the inspiration of Japanese art. At the same time, he expands the perspective of the Glasgow School from the intimacy of the rural lowlands into expanses of Highland mountain and sky. Yet these are no picture postcards in the mould of McCulloch or Peter Graham, for Cameron was an artist of the new century concerned with problems of abstraction and representation. Such formal concerns are complemented by a subtle Celticism, perhaps most obvious in the watercolours of Iona and the Inner Hebrides he contributed as frontispieces to the collected 'Fiona Macleod' works of the writer William Sharp, published in 1911. Born in Dumbarton the late eighteen fifties, William Strang was very much of the Glasgow School generation, but he never worked in Glasgow, settling in London after studying, like Macgregor, with Legros at the Slade. In London he drew and etched portraits which included those of William Sharp, Thomas Hardy, Rudyard Kipling and Robert Louis Stevenson, and he painted a number of striking works including a well-known portrait of Vita Sackville-West, *Lady with a Red Hat* (1918). But his most significant work is in the form of etchings which echo his socialist convictions and combine Christian imagery with a shadowy, psychoanalytical heaviness which has something in common with the work of his contemporary, the Belgian painter James Ensor (1860–1949). The atmosphere of these etchings can be related to the muted palette of another London-based Scottish artist of the period, James Pryde (1866–1941). Pryde kept in close touch with a number of the Glasgow School, but he explored a quite different aesthetic territory. Perhaps even more than Strang he can be thought of as an artistic equivalent of Robert Louis Stevenson, concerned with the interplay of appearance, motive and desire. He was keenly interested in the theatre and toured Scotland in 1895 with his friend Edward Gordon Craig, and many of his works have the quality of stage sets, not least in their large scale and dramatic lighting. At the same time he pioneered an influential lithographic

115. **William Strang** *Grotesque*, 1897. In the hands of Strang, etching was used both for straightforward illustrative purposes and to explore a psychodynamic territory which owes much to Goya and resonates with Ensor.

116. **James Pryde** *Lumber: A Silhouette*, 1921. Pryde's close association with the theatre is evident in this painting. It evokes a feeling of disquiet which resonates with contemporary Surrealist developments in Paris.

poster style, working along with his brother-in-law, the English painter William Nicholson, under the joint pseudonym of the Beggarstaff Brothers. Pryde's fantasy images tend to involve lonely figures dwarfed by their circumstances. Characteristic is his series from the 1920s which takes as its subject a great four-poster bed at the Palace of Holyroodhouse in Edinburgh, at one time thought to have been that of Mary Queen of Scots. This bed within a room within a palace the occupant of which was long gone, was used by Pryde as a sort of myth-like summary of the human condition in history. His work illuminates a liminal

116

space where meaning can slip as in a dream and it thus forms an intriguing link between between symbolism and surrealism.

Arts, Crafts and Celtic Revival in Edinburgh

In the Glasgow of Francis Newbery and Charles Rennie Mackintosh the Arts and Crafts movement was influential. In Edinburgh it was even more so. Early stirrings of Arts and Crafts ideas in Scotland can be found in the stained-glass revival which began in the 1850s. Very little old Scottish stained glass survived the Reformation and, whatever the irony, this clean sheet enabled Scottish artists of the mid-nineteenth century to develop stained glass as a medium of illustrative vigour. The pioneer was James Ballantine (1808–1877), who began his career as an apprentice to David Roberts and probably trained as a stained-glass artist in Newcastle. His major works include the great west window of Dunfermline Abbey to designs by Joseph Noel Paton, and the scheme of glass for St Giles Kirk in Edinburgh, to designs by Robert Herdman, which was completed by his son, Alexander. William Morris and Edward Burne-Jones also contributed a window to St Giles. In Glasgow the pioneer was Daniel Cottier (1838–1891), who had probably studied with Ballantine and had been directly influenced by Morris, Ford Madox Brown and Ruskin. Cottier made a virtue of the simplification required of the stained-glass artist. Through the work of followers such as Stephen Adam and Adam's son of the same name his stylistic influence became part of the experimental mixture of 1890s Glasgow, most notably in the work of David Gauld and George Walton. Much of this work was secular but there was a parallel history to that of the religious glass. Stephen Adam's *The Glassblower* (1878) can be seen as part of a development of industrial genre imagery. James Guthrie's image of *Vikings at Loch Lomond* (1887) both provides a footnote to Scottish history painting and gives an added dimension to the art of a man better known as one of the leaders of the Glasgow School.

In Edinburgh a number of supporters of Arts and Crafts ideas, keen to link art with social change, were in positions of influence. They included the Professor of Fine Art at Edinburgh University, Gerard Baldwin Brown; the most influential Scottish architect of the day, Robert Rowand Anderson; and the botanist, sociologist and Celtic Revival activist Patrick Geddes, who was the focal point of a remarkable group of artists. Geddes is most remembered today as a pioneer of ecology and sensitive town planning but he stressed that at the heart of any planning process must be an understanding of cultural history both verbal and visual. Evolutionary ideas permeated his thinking and in the cultural sphere these were expressed in terms of the revitalizing and development of local and national traditions. Geddes admired Mackintosh, seeing in his work a clear-sighted and creative understanding of the past and the present which at the same time showed a way forward. In his advocacy of traditional revival as the foundation of future development Geddes is close in his thinking to his fellow advocate of Celtic Revival, the Irish poet W. B. Yeats, and to a poet who was to be in due course a friend of both men, the Indian nationalist Rabindranath Tagore. To further such cultural aims, in 1885 Geddes helped to found the Edinburgh Social Union, an organization imbued with Arts and Crafts social and aesthetic concerns. In 1889 further Arts and Crafts impetus came from the third meeting of the National Association for the Advancement of Art and its Application to Industry, held in Edinburgh. Speakers included Geddes, Francis Newbery, Walter Crane and William Morris himself. The consequences of this gathering were to extend far into the twentieth century. Symbolic of this was the establishment in 1909 of tapestry making at the Dovecot Studio in Edinburgh, under the direction of the artist-designer William Skeoch Cumming (1864–1929) and the patronage of the Marquess of Bute. Other major figures involved were the architect and designer Robert Lorimer (1864–1929), and the stained-glass artist Douglas Strachan (1875–1950).

A central figure in this late flowering of Arts and Crafts was Phoebe Anna Traquair (1852–1936), and one of the first actions of the Edinburgh Social Union was to commission her to paint murals for the Mortuary Chapel of the Sick Children's Hospital in Edinburgh. She was born in Dublin where she met and in 1873 married the Scottish palaeontologist Ramsay Traquair, returning with him to Edinburgh where she worked for the rest of her life. She was influenced by the work of William Morris and the Pre-Raphaelites, and also by the associated example of William Bell Scott and Joseph Noel Paton. A complete craftswoman, she operated at the highest level in media ranging from metalwork through embroidery, bookbinding, illumination and illustration to mural painting. Among her major achievements is the mural scheme for the interior of the Catholic Apostolic Church in Mansfield Place (1893–1901) in Edinburgh. This project, which includes the west wall and the chancel arch of this large church, is breathtaking both in its scale and in its quality. During the same period she produced four embroidered panels of startling quality in silk and gold thread on linen, each about six feet in height,

117. **Phoebe Anna Traquair** *Despair*, 1899–1902. One of a series of four embroidered panels, each over six feet in height, entitled jointly *The Progress of a Soul*. Phoebe Traquair was equally impressive as a mural painter, illuminator, book illustrator, cover designer, and jewellery enamellist. She was an outstanding representative of Arts and Crafts philosophy in practice.

entitled *The Progress of a Soul* (1893–1902). These meditative works would have been among those which led her friend W. B. Yeats to write in 1906, 'I have come from her work, overwhelmed, astonished, as I used to come long ago from Blake and from him alone'. Traquair brought to her work a direct appreciation of medieval and early Renaissance Italian painting, gathered on visits to Tuscany in the company of Alexander and Elizabeth Whyte, and her friendship with the Whytes gives insight into the cultural and religious life of the period. Alexander Whyte was a renowned Free Church theologian particularly noted for his knowledge of Christian mysticism, while his wife Elizabeth was an early advocate of the Baha'i faith, an interest she shared with Patrick Geddes. Phoebe Traquair expressed the religious generalism of the time in the pattern of her church-related commissions. These included, as well as the Catholic Apostolic Church, murals for the Song School of St Mary's Episcopalian Cathedral in Edinburgh and a number of book covers and illustrations for Alexander Whyte, including a roundel portrait of Cardinal Newman for Whyte's selection from that author's work.

Influenced by Traquair was Patrick Geddes' close colleague, John Duncan (1866–1945). Born in Dundee and trained there as

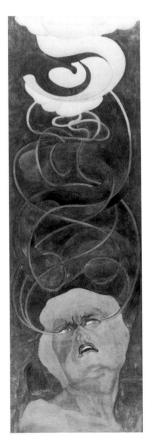

119. **George Dutch Davidson** *Envy*, 1898. The short-lived Davidson shared a studio in Dundee with John Duncan. This work is impressive in its exploration of symbolism.

an illustrator, like Traquair Duncan was inspired by the art of the early Italian Renaissance and frequently used tempera later in his career in homage to those artists. He brought this into direct contact with imagery derived from the Celtic art of the eighth and ninth centuries, often emphasizing this by use of Iona as a background. This blending of Italian influence and Celtic decoration can be seen clearly in works such as *St Bride* (1913) and *The Adoration of the Magi* (1915). In the latter work, East and West are also united not least through the depiction of a Yin Yang symbol, hardly a common sight in European imagery at the time. A few years earlier he had painted *The Riders of the Sidhe* (1911) and *Tristan and Iseult* (1912), works which have since become icons of the Celtic Revival. Duncan owed a significant debt to the example of the French Symbolist painter Pierre Puvis de Chavannes (1824–98), and he can be considered as part of a current of early twentieth-century European Symbolism. This links him to fellow Theosophists like Piet Mondrian (in his early overtly Symbolist phase) and the Russian painter Nicolai Roerich. It is likely that Duncan was aware of Roerich's work for Diaghilev's Ballets Russes in Paris. Indeed the two artists may have met when Duncan, accompanied by his student Eric Robertson, visited J. D. Fergusson in Paris in 1910, for Fergusson was very much part of that dance-orientated Parisian milieu. Other Dundee Symbolists who can be mentioned are Stewart Carmichael (1867–1950) and the short-lived George Dutch Davidson (1879–1901) who shared a studio with Duncan in 1898–99. Davidson's illustrations are of the highest technical and imaginative quality and they provide a stylistic link between Duncan and Glasgow artists such as Jessie M. King and Annie French. This Symbolist current finds later expression in the eccentric work of Ancell Stronach (1901–81).

118

119

John Duncan was one of the leading artists of Patrick Geddes' magazine *The Evergreen* and contributed a visual manifesto of the Celtic Revival, *Anima Celtica* (1895), to the first issue. This image takes the Celticism and the Japanese inspiration of George Henry and E. A. Hornel much further, and these twin influences of Celtic and Japanese art give *The Evergreen* its visual presence. Other artists involved included James Cadenhead (1858–1927), A. G. Sinclair (1859–1930), Charles Mackie (1862–1920), William Walls (1860–1942), W. G. Burn-Murdoch (1862–1939), Robert Burns (1869–1941), Robert Brough (1872–1905), Helen Hay (*fl.* 1895–1953), Alice Gray (*fl.* 1882–1904) and Nellie Baxter (*fl.* 1895). Pittendrigh Macgillivray contributed both graphic works and poetry and it is worth noting in passing that Macgillivray had been first editor of the journal set up by the painters of the Glasgow School a few years before, *The Scottish Art Review*. Among contributors to *The Evergreen* were the renowned collectors of Gaelic poetry in Scotland and Ireland respectively Alexander Carmichael and Douglas Hyde. Another was William Sharp (Fiona Macleod) who also had an editorial role. The women artists involved in the magazine deserve to be better known. Helen Hay in particular is a graphic artist to be valued. Her work is a key part of *The Evergreen* both with respect to her interpretations for modern use of initial letters based on Celtic manuscripts, and in full page almanacs she designed for three of the four issues published. The appearance of one of E. A. Hornel's Japanese works in *The Evergreen* has been mentioned and Mackie, Cadenhead and Burns were particularly responsive to Japanese art. An example of this is Robert Burns's *Natura Naturans* dated prominently 1891, perhaps to emphasize that it is pre-Beardsley in execution, for by the time *The Evergreen* was published Aubrey Beardsley's illustrations for the Dent edition of Malory's *Morte d'Arthur* (1893–94) were widely known.

120

Patrick Geddes had strong links with France and a number of French writers contributed to *The Evergreen* including the anarchist geographer Élisée Reclus. Geddes had a particular interest in Breton culture as part of a wider Celtic Revival and the Brittany-born Post-Impressionist painter Paul Serusier (1863–1927) was represented in *The Evergreen*. Charles Mackie had met Serusier's older colleague Paul Gauguin (1848–1903) in Paris in the early 1890s. He subsequently worked at Pont Aven in Brittany with Serusier and was influenced by the synthesism developed by the Pont Aven painters. This can be seen clearly in his *Evergreen* work. A result of these contacts was that Serusier was invited to design a mural for Ramsay Garden, Patrick Geddes' Arts and Crafts condominium built on Castle Hill in Edinburgh in the 1890s. Ramsay Garden was conceived of as a sort of informal college that combined tenement flats for academics and artists with a self-governing student hall of residence. It was designed by Stewart Henbest Capper and Sydney Mitchell around the eighteenth-century house that had been built by Allan Ramsay the poet and subsequently owned by his son the painter. Ramsay Garden thus had the history of Scottish art and literature at its heart and Geddes exploited this as the basis of his advocacy of cultural revival. A number of murals were painted there but, with the exception of a notable series by John Duncan, little has survived. Serusier's *Evergreen* image, *Pastorale Bretonne* (1895) may well have been intended as a design for one of those murals. An artist whose contribution to *The Evergreen* was probably as much a result of his Breton connections as his Scottish background was Robert Brough. It is thought that Brough first visited Pont Aven in 1894. At this time he had no settled style but some works from this period, including his *Evergreen* image *Roses* (1896), show a synthesist influence. Brough spent his early life in Aberdeen and always kept up links with that city. He studied at the Royal Scottish Academy in Edinburgh and in due course moved to London where he was strongly influenced by the portraiture of John Singer Sargent (1856–1925). Due to his death in his early thirties this eclectic artist never had an opportunity to develop a mature style but his ability as a painter is impressive. His friendship with the colourist Samuel John Peploe leads us on to the next phase of Scottish art.

120. **Robert Burns** *Natura Naturans*, 1891. This work was published in Patrick Geddes' *Evergreen* in 1895. Although part of Geddes' Celtic Revival milieu, Burns here shows his active interest in Japanese art, echoing Hokusai in every wave-form.

121. **S. J. Peploe** *The Black Bottle,*
c. 1905. The influence of Manet is clear
in this early work by Peploe. By this time
Paris was a common place of study for
Scottish painters and Peploe and his
fellow Colourists took full advantage of it.

Chapter 8: Twentieth-Century Pluralism

The Colourists

By the beginning of the twentieth century studying in Paris was the norm for promising Scottish artists. The Glasgow School had set the pattern. It was taken up at the turn of the century by the Edinburgh-based painters Samuel John Peploe (1871–1935), John Duncan Fergusson (1874–1961), and Francis Campbell Boileau Cadell (1883–1937). Along with George Leslie Hunter (1879–1931) these painters are now known as the Scottish Colourists. In their early work they show affinity with Whistler and Manet, for example Fergusson's evocation of fireworks in *Dieppe, Night* (1905) and Peploe's wonderfully articulated still life *The Black Bottle* (1905). The immediate context of their painting is the emphasis on form as dependent on colour that characterized the work of the Glasgow Boys and the late paintings of William McTaggart. They were thus in a strong position to respond to the formal and colouristic developments that took place in Paris in the wake of the Post-Impressionism of Cézanne, Gauguin and Van Gogh. Fergusson's *The Blue Hat* (1909) and Peploe's *Boats at Royan* (1910) show just how powerful that response was. Like Lavery, Peploe studied at both the Académie Julian and the Atelier Colarossi, first travelling to Paris in 1894 in the company of his friend and fellow student at the Royal Scottish Academy schools, Robert Brough. In the latter half of the decade both Fergusson and Cadell studied in Paris and the new century saw Fergusson and Peploe working there together. In the years after 1905 both Fauvism and Cubism were developing and Peploe, Fergusson and Cadell absorbed these influences, in particular the experimental Colourism of painters such as Henri Matisse (1869–1964) and André Derain (1880–1954). Hunter had a somewhat different experience. He spent his youth in California and was inspired to paint by a visit to Paris in 1904. Subsequently, he was encouraged by Alexander Reid in Glasgow, meeting Fergusson in Paris in 1914. Other Scottish artists in Paris at the time included Jessie M. King and her husband E. A. Taylor (1874–1951). Paris had thus assumed an importance for Scottish artists comparable to

121

122

that of Rome in the time of Gavin Hamilton. It was to keep that importance until after the Second World War.

While Peploe, Cadell and Hunter remained based in Scotland in 1907 Fergusson's long visits to Paris became permanent residence. In 1909 he was elected a Sociétaire of the Salon d'Automne and his immediate circle included the French Fauve painters Othon Friesz (1879–1949) and André Dunoyer de Segonzac (1884–1974), the Dutch painter Kees van Dongen (1877–1968), and the American painter Anne Estelle Rice (1879–1959). This was the Paris of Isadora Duncan and the Ballets Russes and dance and the associated designers were influential on the Colourists. It was also the Paris of Bergson's philosophical analysis of time and in 1913 Proust's literary response to it. As part of this intellectual and artistic milieu Fergusson's painting became an explicit investigation of the rhythmical unity of space and time. In 1911 he painted a boldly delineated female nude in the role of Eve entitled *Rhythm* and this gave its title to an avant-garde magazine edited in London by Middleton Murry, Michael Sadleir and Katherine Mansfield. The first cover is based on Fergusson's painting and under his direction as art editor *Rhythm* published the work of an impressive list of artists which included Picasso, Derain, Marquet, Frieze and Gaudier-Brzeska as well as Peploe, Rice and Fergusson himself. In the years between 1910 and 1913 Fergusson painted his most important work of the period, *Les Eus*, in some sense a 123 response to Matisse's *La Danse* (1910). But where Matisse pursues a fluidity of form, Fergusson, in his linear, rhythmic and sensual treatment of these naked dancers at one with the forest, is precise in a way that echoes Poussin's *Bacchanalian Revel* on the one hand and Hindu temple sculpture on the other. A didactic quality of this work is underlined by the title which relates to the linking of gesture and emotion systematized in the Eurhythmic theories of Jaques-Dalcroze and Rudolf Steiner. In 1913 Margaret Morris, the American who was to become a pioneer of modern dance in Britain, became Fergusson's lifelong partner. This commitment to the body in movement is not echoed in the work of the other Colourists, although from about 1913 Cadell became a distinguished painter of single figures in interior settings, uniting a Parisian painterliness with the insights of his older friend John Lavery. In the twenties Cadell developed figure compositions and still lifes as formalized, hard-edged patterns of flat colour 124 which on the one hand echo the qualities of Art Deco and on the other prefigure abstraction.

122. **J. D. Fergusson** *The Blue
Hat, Closerie des Lilas*, 1909.
Along with Peploe, Cadell and
Hunter, Fergusson was strongly
interested by the experiments in
colour and form to be found in the
work of Matisse and the Fauves.

123. (below) **J. D. Fergusson**
Les Eus, *c*. 1910–13. Fergusson's
involvement with the dance
culture of Paris is evident in
this work. In 1913 he met the
American pioneer of modern
dance Margaret Morris, who
became his lifelong partner.

A less obvious aspect of the work of the Colourists is its link to the Celtic Revival. For Cadell and Peploe this was largely a matter of place, for Fergusson it was a question of ideas. In 1912 Cadell had begun to visit Iona and in 1920, he was joined in his annual visits by Peploe. In this they followed in the footsteps of William Bell Scott and John Duncan, and discovered again the clarity of west-coast light that McTaggart had taken for granted. Together in the 1920s and 1930s they painted numerous Iona works which have an enviable directness of touch. A common subject was the view across to Ben More on Mull of which both men painted a number 126 of versions. John Duncan was still active and while he maintained his interest in Celtic legend, he painted a number of straightfor-ward landscapes late in his career which are stylistically close to those of Peploe and Cadell. It has already been noted that Duncan had visited J. D. Fergusson in Paris in 1910 and while *Les Eus* owes

124. **F. C. B. Cadell** *Still Life (The Grey Fan)*, c. 1920–25 Although well-known for portraits and interiors of subtle tonality, it can be seen in this still life that Cadell later developed a hard-edged style bordering on abstraction.

125. **Stanley Cursiter** *Rain on Princes Street*, 1913. Cursiter, in due course Director of the National Galleries of Scotland and a strong advocate of a gallery of modern art for Scotland, here contributes a moment of Futurism to Scottish art.

much to the Fauvism of Paris, it also has a debt to the decorative art of Duncan's Edinburgh. In *Les Eus* Fergusson combined the closed rhythms of Celtic design and the colourism of the Fauves. He wrote later that 'if Scotland, or Celtic Scotland, would make a "new alliance" with France, not political like the "auld alliance" but cultural, it would perhaps put Scotland back on to the main track of her culture'. In these words one almost hears the voice of Patrick Geddes, for Fergusson emphasizes the significance of traditional culture within a contemporary international context, just as Geddes would have done. A younger artist who, like Fergusson, drew on knowledge of Celtic art in a modernist context was Stanley Cursiter (1887–1976). While Fergusson's work has something in common with the contemporary development of Futurism in Italy, Cursiter was directly influenced by that style. He was born at Kirkwall in Orkney and educated not in Paris but at the newly opened Edinburgh College of Art. In 1909 he contributed Celtic Revival decorations to *The Orkney Book* and in 1911

126. **S. J. Peploe** *Ben More from Iona*, 1925. Following the path trodden by Celtic revival artists such as John Duncan, Peploe – and before him Cadell – travelled often to Iona to paint. The result was a memorable and vivid body of colourist work from both artists.

he saw Futurist work at the Grafton Gallery in London. Thanks to introductions to Roger Fry and Clive Bell, Cursiter was instrumental in bringing Post-Impressionist and Futurist work to the Society of Scottish Artists exhibition in Edinburgh the next year. His interest in Futurism resulted in notable works such as *Rain on Princes Street* (1913) and *The Regatta* (1913). As with Fergusson, in both works a strong decorative sense underpins visual experimentation. Cursiter went on to have a distinguished career both as a painter of the Orcadian coastline and as Director of the National Galleries of Scotland. The moment of Futurism in his work found little echo in his later paintings but it gave him a direct insight into the modern movement. This informed Cursiter's thought not least in his proposal in 1930 for a Scottish National Gallery of Modern Art.

The landscape vision of Peploe, Cadell and Hunter was to be highly influential on later Scottish painters. Complementing the west-coast work of Peploe and Cadell, Hunter was a brilliant observer of the quality of inland Scottish light, where green assumes a heavy vividness. From the 1920s he used a subdued but

125

127. **G. L. Hunter** *Houseboats, Balloch*, c. 1924. A further example of the Fauve-influenced imagination of the Colourists. Here the example of Parisian art is interpreted in terms of the comparatively subdued sunlight typical of inland Scotland.

vibrant palette to create a number of notable paintings around Balloch on Loch Lomond. At the same time strong links were maintained with France in the inter-war years, Peploe and Cadell for example painting frequently at Cassis, a location favoured also by John Maclauchlan Milne (1886–1957) who likewise shared the older painters' commitment to the west coast of Scotland. Complementing their landscape works Peploe, Hunter and Cadell explored form and colour systematically through still lifes, which share a clear origin in Cézanne's analytical commitment to that genre. These were as influential on succeeding generations of Scottish painters as were their landscapes and much of this influence was communicated through Aitken Dott's Scottish Gallery in Edinburgh, a gallery which had consistently supported McTaggart and had a significance for Edinburgh comparable to that of Alexander Reid for Glasgow. Peploe, who was invited to teach there in 1933, communicated Colourism directly to students at Edinburgh College of Art. This invitation to him to pass on his skills late in life says much about the esteem in which his work was held.

127

The Edinburgh Group

The early years of the twentieth century saw the pattern of teaching institutions within Scotland begin to assume its modern shape as the diverse possibilities available in each of Scotland's four cities became focused on single institutions. Glasgow had led the way here in the mid-nineteenth century. In the latter years of the century Aberdeen and Dundee had followed suit. In Edinburgh classes at the Royal Institution gave way in 1909 to Edinburgh College of Art. These schools gave artists the opportunity to study within Scotland in a more systematic way than had ever been possible before. They were complemented by the establishment of Hospitalfield near Arbroath as an place of residential study, thanks to the bequest of Patrick Allan-Fraser in 1890. The establishment of the College of Art reinvigorated teaching in Edinburgh. Among appointments to the staff were Robert Burns and the English painter Henry Lintott (1877–1965). Along with Stanley Cursiter, early students included David Macbeth Sutherland (1883–1973), Alick Sturrock (1885–1953), Eric Robertson (1887–1941), Cecile Walton (1891–1956) and Dorothy Johnstone (1892–1980). Outside the college a popular gathering point for these students was John Duncan's studio in Torphichen Street, and the older painter passed on his linear, symbolist style of drawing to Robertson and Walton in particular. Along with J. G. Spence Smith (1880–1951), John R. Barclay (1884–1964) and William Oliphant Hutchison (1889–1970) but with the exception of Cursiter, they exhibited as 'The Edinburgh Group' which found its mature form when reconstituted in 1919. A further member of the group was Glasgow-educated Mary Newbery, daughter of Francis and Jessie Newbery and a close friend of Cecile Walton, who was herself the daughter of the Glasgow School painter E. A. Walton. Most of the group produced their important work in the years before, during and after the First World War. Later D. M. Sutherland and W. O. Hutchison became distinguished teachers, being appointed to head Gray's School of Art in Aberdeen and Glasgow School of Art respectively.

Eric Robertson developed an overtly sensual version of John Duncan's approach to the nude in works such as *Love's Invading* (1919), which shows an interest in dance shared with Fergusson. Experience in the war led Robertson to attempt to unite the spiked forms of Vorticism with his approach to the nude figure. *Despair* (1921) is one of many attempts throughout Europe to remake art in the psychological aftermath of catastrophe and Robertson's work from this period occupies a space between Expressionism

128. **Eric Robertson** *Love's Invading*, 1919. The symbolism of John Duncan had a direct but more sensual successor in that of Eric Robertson. Along with other members of the Edinburgh group, most of whom were students at the newly established Edinburgh College of Art, Robertson was a regular visitor to Duncan's studio.

128

and Surrealism. His paintings also echo his turbulent personal life. He had married Cecile Walton in 1914 but the marriage failed in 1923. Like Robertson, Cecile Walton drew with great skill, building on the work of John Duncan and the Glasgow Style illustrators. She is most remembered for *Romance* (1920), a remarkable self-portrait which is an ironic commentary on both motherhood and

129. **Cecile Walton** *Romance*, 1920. In this self-portrait, a reworking of Manet's *Olympia* and Titian's *Venus of Urbino*, Cecile Walton makes an ironic comment on the place of women artists in the early twentieth century.

130. (opposite) **Dorothy Johnstone** *September Sunlight*, 1916. Along with Cecile Walton and Eric Robertson, Johnstone was a key member of the Edinburgh group. Her portraits show a superb grasp of how natural light is modulated by interiors. Her ability led to an appointment to teach at Edinburgh College of Art as soon as she graduated.

the history of art. It shows the unclothed artist in the pose of Manet's *Olympia*, not long after the birth of her second child whom she holds, while her first-born looks on quizzically. Women artists were becoming increasingly prominent in Edinburgh at this time. Dorothy Johnstone's talent had reflected in her appointment to the staff of Edinburgh College of Art in 1914 but as a woman she was required to give up teaching work on her marriage to D. M. Sutherland ten years later. Without the stimulus of teaching her work began to lose impetus but at her best Johnstone painted women and girls with a fluent humanity, which has rarely been equalled. She shares her clarity of vision and understanding of the fall of light with Norah Neilson Gray (1882–1906) who had been taught by Francis Newbery and Jean Delville and at Glasgow School of Art in the early years of the century.

130

The Scottish National War Memorial

The inclusion of Mary Newbery, an applied artist, in the Edinburgh Group indicates the continuing respect for Arts and Crafts in Scotland. In the 1920s this tradition found extraordinary expression in the construction of Robert Lorimer's Scottish National War Memorial (1924–27) within Edinburgh Castle. A statement

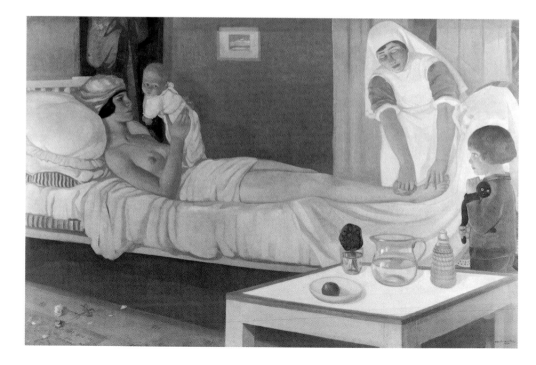

of both national loss and national pride, it was described at the time as a *coronach* (that is to say a lament) in stone. It provided magnificent opportunities for sculptors, most of whom were associated with Edinburgh College of Art. They included Percy Portsmouth (1874–1953), Alice Meredith Williams (1880–1934) and her husband Morris (1881–1973), Alexander Carrick (1882–1966), Pilkington Jackson (1887–1973) and Phyllis Bone (1894–1972). The stained glass was the work of the renowned designer Douglas Strachan who had set up the stained-glass 133 studio at Edinburgh College of Art when it opened. This major project stamped the development of twentieth-century Scottish sculpture with an Arts and Crafts outlook which carried on at Edinburgh College of Art through Alexander Carrick's students Tom Whalen (1903–75) and Hew Lorimer (1907–73). The latter came from a family of artists and architects. His father was Robert Lorimer and his uncle, John Henry Lorimer (1856–1936), had painted the notable *Ordination of the Elders* in 1891. Hew had intended to be an architect like his father, but influenced by Carrick he turned to sculpture. He went on to study with Eric Gill in England and, like Gill, he became a Roman Catholic. Among a number of remarkable works of public sculpture is *Our Lady of* 132 *the Isles* (1954–56), a granite statue twenty-seven feet in height looking out across the Atlantic from South Uist. J. D. Fergusson had from 1908 onwards made a series of sculptures which are very much part of the modern movement. These include *Eastre* 131 *(Hymn to the Sun)* (1924) in polished brass and a number of stone carvings. In the years before the First World War Glasgow School of Art found a sculpture student attuned to recent figurative developments. Estonian-born Benno Schotz (1891–1984) had originally come to Glasgow to study engineering at John Brown's shipyard. Influenced by Rodin, Mestrovic and Epstein, he was one of a notable group of Glasgow School of Art students who attended towards the end of Francis Newbery's period as Director. In due course Schotz became an influential portrait sculptor. At his best he equals Epstein, whom he engagingly refers to in his autobiography as 'my elder brother'. Appropriately enough, one of Schotz's earliest works was a portrait in old age of Pittendrigh Macgillivray. A close contemporary of Schotz who must be mentioned was the Montrose sculptor William Lamb (1893–1951), who produced distinguished figure and portrait work in the interwar years.

132. **Hew Lorimer** *Our Lady of the Isles*, 1954–56. The artist is seen here working on the maquette of the statue which in its full-scale granite version stands more than twenty-five feet high, overlooking the Atlantic from South Uist.

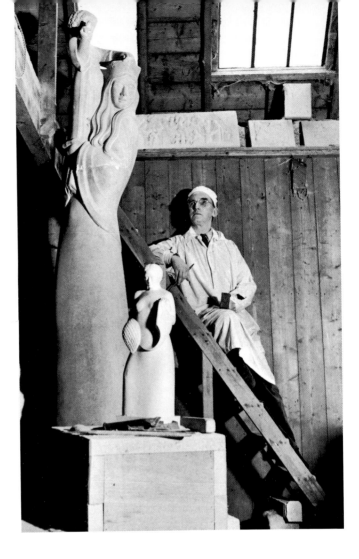

Overleaf:
133. **Douglas Strachan** *Cain*, c. 1927. The Arts and Crafts tradition in Scotland found a twentieth-century focus in the project for the Scottish National War Memorial at Edinburgh Castle, completed in 1927. Integral to the building by Robert Lorimer is a major scheme of stained glass by Douglas Strachan, a detail of which is shown here.

134. **James Cowie** *Self-portrait: The Blue Shirt*, 1945–50. Aware of the precursors of his own dispassionate symbolism, Cowie shows himself with reference to Poussin and Clouet.

James Cowie and his Influence

Among Benno Schotz's friends at Glasgow School of Art were the painters James Cowie (1886–1956), Robert Sivell (1888–1974) and Archibald McGlashan (1888–1980). Cowie is the most important of these. He was born in Aberdeenshire and studied at the United Free Church Training College in Aberdeen, where he was encouraged by the art master, James Hector. He finally reached Glasgow School of Art in 1912 at the relatively late age of twenty-six. There he came into contact with the teaching of the Belgian painter Maurice Grieffenhagen (1862–1931) and the English painter Frederick Cayley Robinson (1862–1927). Cayley Robinson was

171

Thy brothers blood crieth
unto me from the ground

133, 134. Captions on
previous page.

inspired, like John Duncan, by both Pre-Raphaelitism and Puvis
de Chavannes and these influences were passed on to Cowie. In
addition to this Cowie brought to his art a depth of understanding
of classical and neo-classical art. In 1914 he was appointed art
master of Bellshill Academy. There he painted a number of images
of schoolgirls in interiors that have a passing resemblance to

Dorothy Johnstone's work. But where Johnstone is warmly involved with her subjects and her paint, Cowie is distanced, fascinated by the other world of the school art room which he evokes through careful delineation of form and suppression of brushstrokes. There is an elegiac quality to his work, which links it to that of the Pre-Raphaelites. One of his paintings, *Falling Leaves* (1934) in which he explores the passing of girlhood into adolescence, is a deliberate successor to Millais' *Autumn Leaves*. Such placing of his own work with reference to the history of art is found again in his late *Self-portrait: The Blue Shirt* (1945–50). There he bases his composition on Poussin's self-portrait in the Louvre and reproduces in the background the same artist's *Inspiration of the Poet* and Clouet's *Diane de Poitiers*. The layered references of Cowie's realism leave it only a small step from the surrealism of Delvaux and Magritte. In the 1940s he painted *Evening Star* (1943–44) and *Noon* (1947), images of fragmented classical sculpture and classicized figures. These are explorations of fragmentation of knowledge, memory and history which prefigure the concerns of Postmodernism. Cowie had a considerable

134

135. (opposite) **James McIntosh Patrick** *Traquair House*, 1938. Before the Second World War Patrick painted landscapes which hint at the surreal while drawing on a tradition of northern European painting stemming from Bruegel.

influence on painters of the next generation such as Edward Baird and James McIntosh Patrick, and he continued to be influential on younger artists in his role as Warden of Hospitalfield from 1936.

James McIntosh Patrick (1907–98) was born in Dundee and painted there most of his life, but he was trained at Glasgow School of Art. In Glasgow he and Montrose-born Edward Baird (1904–49) were both strongly influenced by the alternative to the Colourists offered by occasional contact with Cowie's work. The tradition of illustrative symbolism in Dundee, which can be seen in the work of John Duncan, George Dutch Davidson and Stewart Carmichael, would have made these artists particularly receptive to Cowie's approach. A number of McIntosh Patrick's landscapes from the 1930s echo Cowie's interiors in the inspiration they take from the history of European art. Bruegel was of particular importance and landscapes like *Traquair House* (1938) have a sharply 135 defined detachment combined with an ominous treatment of light, which as with Cowie's work edges towards Surrealism. These aspects were to drop away in McIntosh Patrick's post-war art in favour of a rural contentment. His friend Edward Baird spent most of his forty-five years in his native Montrose and Baird adopts an overtly surreal approach in works such as *The Birth of Venus* (1934). This atmosphere was maintained in paintings such as *Unidentified Aircraft* (1942) which shows three upturned faces and 136 a hand almost dismembered by the frame. Behind is a stark vision of Montrose on a snowy moonlit night, which again brings Bruegel to mind. In this work Baird summed up the sense of

136. **Edward Baird** *Unidentified Aircraft (over Montrose)*, 1942. McIntosh Patrick's friend Baird contributed to an east-coast school of northern European inspiration with this evocation of the uneasy atmosphere of wartime. Central to the composition is his home town of Montrose.

suspended reality that characterizes war. Bruegel is also an important influence on the early work of another artist from the north-east, Aberdeen-educated Alberto Morocco (1917–98) in works like *A Winter Morning* (1951). McIntosh Patrick originally made his name as an etcher, on occasion painting and etching the same scenes as in *Stobo Kirk* (1936). Here he is a link to the work of two leading printmakers who came to prominence in the 1930s, William Wilson (1905–72) and Ian Fleming (1906–94). Wilson had studied stained glass in the workshop of James Ballantine (grandson of the pioneering stained-glass artist of the same name) and went on to create outstanding work in that medium. As a printmaker he studied etching at Edinburgh College of Art while Fleming pursued a similar course at Glasgow. In the early 1930s they both made works which seem to encapsulate the experience of Scottish printmakers over the previous two centuries. Etchings such as Wilson's *North Highland Landscape* (1934) and *St Monance* (1937), and Fleming's engraving *Gethsemane* (1931) have a rare beauty and command of the medium. Fleming went on to become Principal of Gray's School of Art and in due course a very fine print studio, Peacock Printmakers, was established in Aberdeen.

Experimental Landscape

Living in England during the First World War, J. D. Fergusson had painted a number of Cubist- and Vorticist-influenced images of warships in various states of repair at Portsmouth Docks. In London he made common cause with Charles Rennie Mackintosh and the English critic Frank Rutter in an attempt to start a London Salon of The Independents (on the model of the French Salon des Indépendants of the 1880s). That came to nothing but Fergusson's knowledge of the south of France must have been a factor in the decision by Mackintosh and Margaret Macdonald to settle at Port Vendres in 1923. As support for Mackintosh's architectural work had waned, architecture's loss had become painting's gain, for in the 1920s he produced a number of extraordinary images of landscape, among them *Mont Alba* (*c.* 1924–27). 140

139. **D. Y. Cameron** *Wilds of Assynt,* 1936. Cameron's immense project of painting the Highlands in its analytical approach to landscape shares something with the later work of Charles Rennie Mackintosh.

These watercolours are often seen as the unique creation of a unique artist but Mackintosh's links with Fergusson allow one to see them in a different light, for the analytical way in which the two artists approach landscape is not dissimilar. Fergusson brought the rhythmic insights of his figure painting to his landscapes of the inter-war years. A number of these works were made in the Highlands, for example *Craigcornach* (*c.* 1925) which Frank Rutter reproduced in the 1930s in his influential popular work *Modern*

Masterpieces. This analytical approach to landscape finds earlier expression and contemporary echoes in work by D. Y. Cameron, for example his *Wilds of Assynt* (1936). Through Fergusson and Mackintosh an experimental landscape tradition can be seen developing. Their approach was complemented by an attempt to synthesize modernist trends by William McCance (1894–1970). Trained at Glasgow School of Art, McCance moved to London in 1920 with his wife and fellow Glasgow student, the wood-engraver Agnes Miller Parker (1895–1980). There he was influenced by Vorticism and this aspect of his work can be seen in works such as *Mediterranean Hill Town* (1923) and *Joseph Brewer* (1925). His other activities included the running of the Gregynog Press in Wales and the writing of art criticism. As William Hardie has pointed out, in his writing McCance stresses the desirability of uniting the emotional possibilities of Expressionism and the dispassionate analysis of Cubism and his paintings should be seen in this light. As a critic he was particularly appreciated by Jacob Epstein, for McCance was a staunch defender of the sculptor's work in the late thirties when it was under vicious attack. Epstein valued McCance's writing to such an extent that two complete articles are reprinted in his autobiography. Something of the reach of McCance's criticism comes through in a piece from 1937 concerning Epstein's *Consummatum Est* in which he makes an illuminating comparison between Epstein's work and pibroch, the

139

141

140. **Charles Rennie Mackintosh**
Mont Alba, c.1924–27.
Mackintosh's late watercolours of the land forms and settlements near his home in the south of France, are perhaps the most fascinating landscapes painted in Europe in the 1920s.

141. William McCance
Mediterranean Hill Town, 1923.
Cubist and Vorticist influences are
very clear in McCance's work. He
was both an innovative artist and
a respected critic whose writings
in defence of Jacob Epstein in the
1930s were particularly valued
by the sculptor.

great music of the Highland pipes. He concludes his piece with the
prophetic words: 'Leave Epstein alone and your children will bless
you in years to come. Strangle him by abuse and receive the immediate blessings of Dr Goebbels and his band of tenth-rate reporters
in paint and plaster who are leading a nation to cultural suicide.'

McCance's work in the 1920s was admired by Hugh MacDiarmid,
and the poet's radical modernist perception is reflected in the fact
that the other Scottish artist whom he had most regard for was
William Johnstone (1897–1981). The years before 1920 had seen
the publication of two seminal scientific texts by Scottish academics, both of which made extensive use of visual methods: Patrick
Geddes' *Cities in Evolution* (1915) and *On Growth and Form* (1917)

142. William Johnstone
A Point in Time, 1929–38.
Johnstone went from Edinburgh College of Art to study in Paris, where he became interested in the work of the Surrealists. Soon after he worked in America. In this painting he began to evolve a landscape of the unconscious which has something in common with contemporary work by Georgia O'Keeffe.

by D'Arcy Thompson. William Johnstone's paintings of the late 1920s, *A Point in Time* and *Ode to the North Wind*, are very much part of this *Zeitgeist* for, like the science of Geddes and Thompson, Johnstone's art explores evolutionary processes: geological, biological and cultural. Johnstone was the son of a Borders farmer and was fascinated as a child not only by the land itself but by the stone-age implements of cultivation and hunting turned up by the plough. He was encouraged in his desire to become an artist by the Borders landscape painter Tom Scott (1854–1927), and after attending Edinburgh College of Art he studied at the studio of André Lhote in Paris. There Johnstone was open to Lhote's Cubism but also to other influences including Surrealism. Among his friends was the Catalan sculptor Julio Gonzalez (1876–1942), twenty years his senior. His companion, whom he married, was the American sculptor Flora Macdonald who had studied in Edinburgh with Carrick and in Paris with Giacometti. The couple spent the last years of the 1920s in California and Johnstone's work from this period has a distinct similarity to the work of the American painters Georgia O'Keeffe (1887–1986) and Arthur Dove (1880–1946). Johnstone's close contemporary, the short-lived William Crozier (1897–1930), pursued an identical educational course studying at Edinburgh College of Art and then under Lhote in Paris. His *Edinburgh from Salisbury Crags* (1927) reappropriated the perspectives of Alexander Nasmyth in the light of Lhote's decorative Cubism and its influence can be seen in

142

143

143. **William Crozier** *Edinburgh from Salisbury Crags*, 1927. The influence of Crozier's teacher in Paris, André Lhote is clear in this late-Cubist interpretation of Edinburgh.

North Bridge and Salisbury Crags (*c.* 1934) by his elder contemporary Adam Bruce Thomson (1885–1976). Crozier's fellows at Edinburgh College of Art included William Gillies (1898–1973), John Maxwell (1905–1962) and William MacTaggart (1903–1981), grandson of the earlier painter of the same name. Along with the slightly older Donald Moodie (1892–1963), Anne Redpath (1895–1965) and William Geissler (1896–1963), they were central to the development of the Edinburgh School of painting which dominated Scottish art between the wars. Maxwell and Gillies were close friends and when the former painted landscapes, as in *View from a Tent* (1933), their styles are equally close, but Maxwell was in the main exploring a different realm of imagery. David McClure (1926–98), himself a follower of Maxwell, puts it like this: 'fecundity... to Gillies may have been a harvest field bordered by trees in full foliage...to Maxwell she was an earth-goddess with garlands in her hair or some other potent transfiguration.' Maxwell thus picks up on the mythological space explored by John Duncan and brings to it an imagery that owes something to Marc Chagall. For Gillies this was a time of impressive development. In the 1920s he had travelled in France and Italy with Crozier and in the 1930s he travelled in Scotland, often with Maxwell, in a systematic exploration of geography in art. Gillies had a rare ability to absorb influences and make them his own, whether the influence was Bonnard, Peploe, Braque, Nash or Munch. It's difficult to give priority to any one influence but an exhibition of works by Edvard Munch, organized at MacTaggart's prompting at the Society of Scottish Artists exhibition in 1931, certainly made a strong impression. Gillies' works from the 1930s around Ardmurchan and Morar are a *tour de force* in both oil and watercolour, in which the close link between abstraction and landscape is demonstrated. Gillies is often contrasted with his fellow student William Johnstone. They were certainly very different in character yet looking at the experimental freedom of a Gillies oil painting such as *Rocks and Water, Morar* (*c.* 1932–34), one is put in mind of Johnstone's abstract, gestural, ink-wash drawing from a few years later, *Ettrick Raining* (*c.* 1936). But while Johnstone followed this abstracting path after the Second World War, Gillies remained firmly within the confines of representational landscape painting. Both men became

144

144. **W. G. Gillies** *Skye Hills from Near Morar*, *c.* 1931. Often travelling and camping in the company of John Maxwell, Gillies produced a geography of Scotland in art. His watercolours from the 1930s owe something to Munch who had made a selection of his own work for the Society of Scottish Artists in 1931.

145. **William Johnstone**
Celebration of Earth, Air, Fire and Water, 1974. Johnstone's
painting reached its zenith
[aft]er he retired as principal of
[Centr]al School of Arts and Crafts
[in Londo]n. In late works such
[as this he] further explored the
[theme] of ideas of growth
[and lan]dscape which
[engrossed] his early

influential teachers, Gillies as head of the School of Painting and
Drawing at Edinburgh College of Art (subsequently principal),
Johnstone south of the Border as principal successively of two major
London art schools, Camberwell and, after the war, Central.
Johnstone's substantial work as an educator slowed his output as a
painter but on his retirement to the Borders in 1960 he brought to
fruition much of what had been inherent in his work from the 1930s
and 1940s. Perhaps the finest of all these late works is *Celebration of
Earth, Air, Fire and Water* (1974), which is linked directly to the land-   145
scape of the Borders by its implied horizon, for all that it echoes the
non-figurative calligraphic concerns of Abstract Expressionism.

Glasgow in the 1930s and 1940s

A contemporary of Gillies and Johnstone who was also had an
illustrious career as a teacher was Hugh Adam Crawford
(1898–1982). He had begun to teach at Glasgow School of Art in
1925 and he was later appointed head of Gray's School of Art in

Aberdeen and subsequently principal of Duncan of Jordanstone College in Dundee. The interest of his own work is considerable; for example, *Theatre* (c. 1935), displays an understanding of contemporary work by Paul Klee. Crawford is better known as a figurative painter and, like his then colleague at Glasgow School of Art, Ian Fleming, he painted notable wartime works including *Homage to Clydebank* after the catastrophic bombing of 1941. The 1930s saw Crawford influencing the education of a group of students at Glasgow School of Art, which included William Crosbie (1915–99), Robert MacBryde and Robert Colquhoun. As early as 1934, Crosbie had shown precocious talent in the remarkable *Heart Knife*, employing flat, curved forms which show an awareness of Ben Nicholson's work and prefigure the imagery of the English Constructivist-Surrealist John Tunnard. Crosbie went on to study with Léger in Paris and was influenced by him in the formal language he developed for mural commissions from the 1940s onwards. Among his work from the post-war period is *Post Mortem* (c. 1950), which echoes in oil paint the gravity of Epstein's *Consummatum Est*.

J. D. Fergusson and Margaret Morris had moved from the south of France to Glasgow just before the outbreak of the Second

146. **Hugh Adam Crawford** *Theatre*, c. 1935. Although he is better known for his figurative work, Crawford's awareness of the contemporary work of Klee in the 1930s gives some indication of his outstanding value as a teacher to students at Glasgow School of Art before and during the Second World War.

World War and this was an important impetus for Scottish artists. Fergusson was closely involved with the publisher William MacLellan, who made available the artist's challenging book *Modern Scottish Painting* in 1943. William Crosbie also made a major contribution as an illustrator for MacLellan, not least to Sorley Maclean's important early collection of poems *Dain do Eimhir/Songs to Eimhir*. Fergusson was art editor and cover designer of *Scottish Art and Letters*, a remarkable journal which from 1944 included work by leading writers such as Hugh MacDiarmid and Sidney Goodsir Smith, alongside critical assessment of artists ranging from Giorgio de Chirico and Henri Rousseau to Melville, Gillies, MacTaggart and Maxwell. Reproduced in an issue marking the PEN conference at the Edinburgh Festival of 1950 is

147. **William Crosbie** *Heart Knife*, 1934. A brilliant exercise drawing on both Surrealism and Constructivism by the young William Crosbie. It heralded a distinguished career, not least as an illustrator and mural painter.

148. **Donald Bain** *Children of Llyr*, 1945. Along with Crosbie, Bain contributed to *Scottish Art and Letters* of which J. D. Fergusson was art editor. In Children of Llyr the conjunction of Modernism and Celticism which typified this publication can be seen clearly, for the subject of this work is a Celtic legend.

Douglas Young's poem in memory of his fellow poet William Soutar. The poem is integrated into a Celtic Revival knotwork design by George Bain (1881–1968), whose pioneering analysis of the forms of Celtic art of the seventh to ninth centuries was also published by MacLellan. This again draws attention to the link between the art of the Celtic Revival of the 1890s and the Celtic modernism of the mid-twentieth century. Along with Fergusson, artists closely involved with *Scottish Art and Letters* included Andrew Taylor Elder (1908–66) and Donald Bain (1904–79). These artists were also members of the New Scottish Group which had been established in 1942 with Fergusson and the Polish refugee artists Josef Herman and Jankel Adler at its core. Other artists involved in this group included Tom Macdonald (1914–85), Louise Annand (b. 1915) and Bet Low (b. 1924). The younger artists of the New Scottish Group thus connect back to the art of the beginning of the century through Fergusson and this further illuminates his significance for Scottish art over half a century.

148

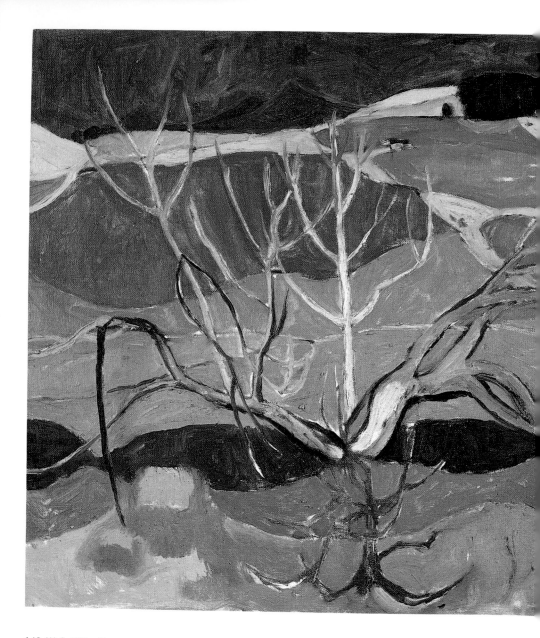

149. **W. G. Gillies** *Mauve
Landscape*, *c*. 1956. Gillies'
painting continued to develop
throughout his career. His
later work, along with that of
MacTaggart and Redpath, opened
the way for a new generation of
landscape painters in Scotland.

Post-War Diversity

During and after the Second World War the tradition of painterly Colourism continued in Edinburgh through Gillies, MacTaggart and Redpath, with MacTaggart and Redpath coming into their own as painters of landscape and still life. Although Redpath commonly used vivid hues in way that echoes Cadell, as in *The Indian Rug* (*c.* 1942), in other works she explored a subtle world of tone. In those paintings she conveyed to the viewer that white is the colour that includes all others, whether the subject is a vase of tulips or a Spanish village. Where MacTaggart exploits the lowering contrasts of Munch and Nolde, Redpath hints at Morandi in her understatement. Though committed to representation, both Redpath and MacTaggart experimented with painting as a unified, textured field and in radically simplified responses to landscape and architectural subjects their work links to the much younger Glasgow-trained painter Joan Eardley. At the same time Gillies continued to experiment, producing works of perception and sureness of touch in 1950s and 1960s such as *Wooded Landscape, Blue Tree* (*c.* 1950) and *Mauve Landscape* (*c.* 1956). Gillies' insights gave grounding to artists of the next generation such as Robert Henderson Blyth (1919–70) and the painter who was to succeed Gillies as Head of Drawing and Painting at Edinburgh College of Art, Robin Philipson (1916–92). On his return from war service Philipson engaged in an intriguing synthesis, responding from a Scottish Colourist base to tendencies in post-war art ranging from Pop Art, to Kokoschka and neo-Romanticism. Philipson's myriad

150

151

149

150. **Anne Redpath** *The Indian Rug*, c. 1942. Subtleties of tone and use of vivid colour characterize Redpath's work.

151. William MacTaggart
Wigtown Coast, 1968. Many of MacTaggart's later works explore landscape through overall paint textures which tend towards abstraction. In works such as the one illustrated he also echoes the work of his grandfather of the same name.

influences give a clue to his success as a teacher but the core of his art was a figurative colourism and this was transmitted to and transmuted by students such as John Bellany (b. 1942) and Alexander Moffat (b. 1943). Philipson's most original work lies in his vigorous, symbolic, sometimes anguished images of animals and birds, notably his *Fighting Cocks* series. In due course Elizabeth Blackadder (b. 1931) and John Houston (b. 1930), among others, took this Edinburgh School forward.

In the 1950s following the success of William Crosbie, three more artists who had been students of Hugh Crawford at Glasgow School of Art before and during the war began to make a major impression. These were Robert MacBryde (1913–66), Robert Colquhoun (1914–62) and Joan Eardley (1921–63), all of whom had also benefited from contact with James Cowie at Hospitalfield. Colquhoun and MacBryde moved to London 1941 where they shared a studio with the neo-Romantic artist John Minton and Colquhoun's work in particular has a neo-Romantic landscape emphasis at the time. In 1943 Jankel Adler (1895–1949) moved from Glasgow to share the studio and the Polish artist's jagged reinterpretations of Cubism and his emphasis on the figure had a major effect on both of the two Roberts. In contrast to the direction of travel of Colquhoun and MacBryde, English-born and initially Goldsmiths-educated Joan Eardley made her permanent

152

152. **Robert Colquhoun** *Figures in a Farmyard*, 1953. Along with Robert MacBryde, Colquhoun created a style which draws both on the work of the Polish exile Jankel Adler and on links with the English neo-Romantic artist John Minton.

153. **Joan Eardley** *Wave*, 1961. Joan Eardley gave Scottish landscape painting new energy and direction. Working outside the colourist tradition of Edinburgh, her paintings of the east coast are as remarkable as Gillies' account of the west coast thirty years before.

home in Scotland, and began to explore first Glasgow and subsequently the Kincardineshire coast in a way that contributed to a new vision of Scotland. Her images of Glasgow tenements and children in the streets are of note not least with respect to a sensitivity to graffiti and posters which resonates with the contemporary concerns of Pop Art. In her work at the Kincardineshire village of Catterline, to which she moved in 1956, she committed herself to understanding the sea more than any painter since McTaggart in the 1890s. Rather than just responding to the attraction of the coastline, she painted with the perception of a mariner aware that waves are heavy, fast-moving lumps of water, as able to kill as to support. In this she reinvigorated a maritime trend in Scottish art which found continuing expression through, among others,

153

John Bellany, Fred Stiven (1929–97), Robert Callender (b. 1932), Elizabeth Ogilvie (b. 1946), Ian Hamilton Finlay (b. 1925), Joyce Cairns (b. 1947), George Wyllie (b. 1921), Frances Walker (b. 1930), Will Maclean (b. 1941) and Ian Stephen (b. 1955). The presence of the sea, the quality of light it provided and its capacity to erode was also important to Wilhelmina Barns-Graham (b. 1912). Born in St Andrews she went to St Ives in 1940 at the suggestion of the then principal of Edinburgh College of Art, Hubert Wellington and became a significant member of the St Ives School. A year earlier another former Edinburgh student, Margaret Mellis (b. 1914), had arrived in St Ives with her husband Adrian Stokes. The central figures of the St Ives School, Barbara Hepworth, Ben Nicholson and Naum Gabo also arrived in 1939. Barns-Graham experimented with abstraction and began to perceive the geological structure of the land in a way informed by Constructivism. The textile designer and painter Alastair Morton (1910–1963), was a further Edinburgh connection to Hepworth and Nicholson and his radical abstract compositions from the 1930s reflect this friendship. 154

Colquhoun and MacBryde explored a tradition which found its origin in the Cubism of Picasso, Braque and Gris. A more optimistic development of the same sources can be can be found in the later art of Alberto Morocco. In contrast to these artists who owed

154. **Wilhelmina Barns-Graham**
Rocks, St Mary's, Scilly Isles,
1953. A member of the St Ives
group in Cornwall, Barns-
Graham's awareness of
Constructivist ideas complements
her approach to geology as a
process of rtability and
movement.

so much to the early years of the century, others were helping to forge a new post-war European art. They included William Gear (1916–97) and Stephen Gilbert (b. 1910), who were part of the short-lived but influential COBRA group in Paris (the name comes from the cities of origin of the first members: Copenhagen, Brussels and Amsterdam). Both were born in Fife but pursued very different routes to post-war Paris. Gilbert was Slade-educated and had spent the war in Dublin, while Gear was trained at Edinburgh College of Art and had studied in Paris with Léger just before the war. After war service Gear returned to the French capital in 1947 and Gilbert introduced him to COBRA painters such as Jorn and Constant. The tense, linear abstracting which characterizes the work of COBRA gave direction to both artists. William Gear acted as a link to contemporary European developments for the young

155. **William Gear** *Autumn Landscape, September, 1950*, 1950. The formal assertiveness of Gear's COBRA work is clear in this reproduction even though the vibrant colour contrasts he developed cannot be appreciated.

156. **Alan Davie** *Jingling Space*, 1950. Helped by Willam Gear in Paris to further his European contacts, as the 1950s dawned Davie's work drew both on the mysterious spaces characteristic of his teacher John Maxwell and on contemporary developments in Abstract Expressionism.

Alan Davie (b. 1920) who visited him in Paris while on a travelling scholarship from Edinburgh College of Art in 1948–49. On the same journey Davie went to Venice and was introduced by Peggy Guggenheim to the work of Jackson Pollock and other American Abstract Expressionists. Davie had already absorbed the exploration of fantasy space to be found in the work of his teacher John Maxwell and the combination of these influences can be seen in works such as *Jingling Space* (1950). On his return to Britain Davie was employed by William Johnstone, at that time principal of Central School of Arts and Crafts in London. Like Johnstone, Davie had an interest in Zen calligraphy and the spontaneity demanded by this approach interacted with Davie's improvisatory skills as a jazz saxophonist. He also shared with Johnstone an interest in Scotland's Celtic and prehistoric past, which he united with traditional cultural influences ranging from Jain cosmologies to Carib rock carving, his works displaying dense, intuitively structured patterns of symbols over the next four decades.

156

Johnstone's role in helping Scottish artists establish themselves in London was significant. Along with Davie he employed William Turnbull (b. 1922) and Eduardo Paolozzi (b. 1924). Both had begun their art education in evening classes, Turnbull at Duncan of Jordanstone in his native Dundee before war service, while Leith-born Paolozzi studied at Edinburgh College of Art after suffering – as an Italian-Scot – the cultural irony of brief internment prior to service in the Pioneer Corps. The two met at the Slade after the war and each spent several years in Paris before returning to London. In the 1950s both made sculptures of the highest quality which owe a debt to contact in Paris with Giacometti. Paolozzi's versions of *Icarus* (1957) and Turnbull's *War Goddess* (1956) are primitivistic statements which reflect on the civilized horror of the technological wars of the twentieth century, on the one hand through a mortal who over-reached himself and on the other through a mysterious totemic presence. At the same time in Scotland the sculptor George Innes (1913–70) was experimenting with a pre-Columbian and Cubist-influenced primitivism. As a painter, Turnbull was influenced by American colour field and action painting and he early recognized the growing importance of New York, visiting for the first time in 1957. Paolozzi, in sculptures of agglomerated machine parts, prints and collages, helped to pioneer a European version of Pop Art which in its irony and classical references contrasted markedly with its brash American counterpart. A feeling of cultural disruption and fragmented knowledge is exploited in his work, whether in the screenprint and collage series *Bunk* (1972), or in the massive bronze public sculptures from the 1980s and 1990s. While in the 1950s Paolozzi used the figure of Icarus, in the 1980s the god Hephaestos became central to his work, not only as a symbol but also combined with self-portraiture. In the 1950s Paolozzi had described his occupation as 'the erection of hollow gods', but within that hollowness resonates the human condition, and most of all in the case of Hephaestos: creative, lame, loving, betrayed. The experimentation of Paolozzi and Turnbull prefigured the openness of a younger generation of sculptors to international influences. Among them were Fred Bushe (b. 1931), Bill Scott (b. 1935), Douglas Cocker (b. 1945), and Jake Harvey (b. 1948).

While Davie, Turnbull and Paolozzi all made their careers elsewhere, as did the painter Craigie Aitchison (b. 1926), their contemporary, Ian Hamilton Finlay (b. 1925), developed his art in Scotland. Finlay trained briefly at Glasgow School of Art prior to serving in the army and while enlisted he got to know Colquhoun,

157
158

157. (opposite above) **Eduardo Paolozzi**, *Icarus*, 1957. Although best known as a pioneer of Pop Art in the 1960s, throughout his career Paolozzi has explored the lessons and ambiguities of classical mythology, as in this fragmentary figure of a mortal who flew too close to the sun.

158. (opposite below) **William Turnbull** *War Goddess*, 1956. Turnbull's primitivistic sculptures resonate with those of Paolozzi as both artists used the medium to remake a meaningful art after the Second World War. Both benefitted from the influence of Giacometti in Paris.

MacBryde and Minton in London. He was first known as a poet rather than an artist, but from the outset he recognized the printed or carved word as visual art. He stands aside from any obvious movement yet is at the same time a key figure in Scottish art. Rather than responding directly to the styles of modernism or classicism he makes of them and their ideological concomitants elements in a visual dictionary. In the 1960s he centred his poetical and sculptural activities at Stonypath, a farmhouse above Dunsyre in Lanarkshire. There he made of the hillside and its sources of water a garden of groves and ponds, poetry and stone, formality and wildness. He called this place 'Little Sparta' in an aphoristic opposition to Edinburgh, the neo-classical Athens of the North, a mere twenty miles to the north-east. The further duality of the everyday Stonypath and the classical Little Sparta creates an

159

159. **Ian Hamilton Finlay** *Elegiac Inscription*, 1975. By the upper pool at Little Sparta, carved in stone are the words 'See Poussin Hear Lorrain'. Finlay, working with the stone carver John Andrew, deftly and poetically distinguishes the hard-edged geometry of the paintings of Nicolas Poussin from the gentler poetical space of his seventeenth-century contemporary Claude Lorrain. At the same time he offers to the passer-by a tension between nature and artifice.

160. **John Bellany** *Allegory*, 1964. Interpreting his own background in a Presbyterian fishing village on the east coast, but in the light of a growing post-war challenge to beliefs of all kinds, in the 1960s John Bellany created a remarkable group of paintings of which this allegorical crucifixion is one.

additional generative tension for Finlay. This mirrors the interplay of classical and genre concerns to be found in David Allan and Robert Burns two centuries before, or indeed in the Roman poets Virgil and Ovid, whose *Eclogues* and *Metamorphoses* are constant presences at Little Sparta. All forms of metamorphosis, whether natural, mythical, alchemical, ideological, military or revolutionary, intrigue Finlay and these concerns can be found echoed in installations, printed works and sculpture. Another key element in his work is the sea as symbol and reality and this is a reminder that Finlay lived in Orkney before coming to Dunsyre. For Finlay the naming of a fishing vessel is an act of metamorphosis that makes of a newly built thing a trusted companion. At the same time the bureaucracy of registration letters is subverted by their poetry.

The generation of Alan Davie, Eduardo Paolozzi and Ian Hamilton Finlay, all of whom were born in the 1920s, became established in the 1950s and 1960s and were producing work of the highest quality into the 1990s, concludes the main body of this book. Nevertheless, although space does not allow full

198

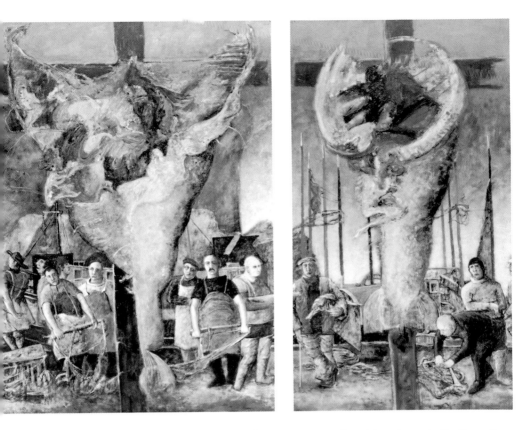

consideration of contemporary Scottish art, an indication of developments and preoccupations up to the time of writing, however incomplete, is desirable.

Epilogue: Deconstructing Stereotypes and Reappropriating Symbols
The importance of the sea to contemporary Scottish artists has been mentioned. Related issues of culture and personal identity were brought out strongly by John Bellany as early as the mid-1960s. His understanding of the psychology of Presbyterian, east-coast fishing communities produced paintings that have a stark and unmistakable authority, such as the crucifixion-based [160] *Allegory* (1964), *Kinlochbervie* (1966) and *Homage to John Knox* (1969). The sea also has a very personal significance for Bellany's near contemporary, Elizabeth Ogilvie. In large paper works such as *Sea Sanctuary* (1989), the artist makes use of material relating to [161] her own forebears from the now-uninhabited island group of St Kilda. Similarly Will Maclean in constructions and prints from the 1970s onwards reflects on loss of maritime skills and the

200

161. (below) **Elizabeth Ogilvie** *Sea Sanctuary*, 1989. Elizabeth Ogilvie's ancestral roots on the now abandoned island of St Kilda, have provided the basis of an art in which the sea becomes a documented aspect of cultural loss.

162. (opposite) **Calum Colvin** *Narcissus*, 1987. In the 1980s Calum Colvin began to use images of well-known works of art as part of his raw material, exploring the nature and veracity of illusion by recreating them from painted domestic objects and interiors.

Gaelic language not as matters of abstract interest but from the standpoint of his own personal experience. These preoccupations resonate with McTaggart's memories of the mid-nineteenth-century Highland clearances recorded in his series of emigrant ship paintings, and Maclean has made the link to the earlier artist explicit in his own *Emigrant Ship* (1992). Related issues of land rights become even more focused in Maclean's remarkable series of memorial cairns in Lewis, completed in the mid-1990s, which mark key events in the struggle for crofting rights up to the 1920s. They use building forms derived from black houses (small dwellings without chimneys) and brochs (circular dry-stone structures) and were undertaken in conjunction with the stonemason James Crawford. This major project marking the political history of the Hebrides gives some indication of how salient issues of culture and identity had become by the 1980s and 1990s. Another aspect of

163

this was a keen interest in the deconstruction of the history of art combined with a critical examination of stereotypes of Scottishness. This can be found in the construction and collage-based photographic work of Ron O'Donnell (b. 1952) and Calum Colvin (b. 1961). Ross Sinclair (b. 1966) has addressed stereotypes both of gender and nation notably in *Fanclub* (1991), a printed postcard of himself against a tartan background with the ambiguous motto: 'All my life I give you nothing and still you ask for more.' Wider identity issues have been addressed in the photographic, video and poetical works of Maud Sulter (b. 1960) who has explored her Glasgow background, her experience as a black woman and the ironies of the classical underpinning of western civilization. Issues of stereotype and reality have been addressed also by the sculptors David Mach (b. 1956) and George Wyllie. The former has made constructions of Irn-Bru bottles filled with Forth

162

164

167

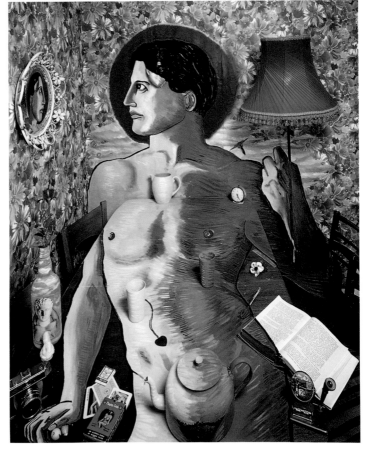

Bridge paint, and the latter's work has running through it a reappropriation of the societal consciousness evident in the poetry
of Robert Burns, Adam Smith's *Theory of Moral Sentiments* and
Adam Ferguson's *Essay on Civil Society*. Further reappropriation
can be found in the work of Kate Whiteford (b. 1952) who has
frequently used symbols of both the Scottish-classical past and the
Scottish-Celtic past. In 1987 Whiteford made a major installation
drawn in marble chips on Calton Hill in Edinburgh which linked   168
classical and Celtic symbolism. It echoes the Enlightenment
columns of the National Monument with concentric arcs reminiscent of the seating of an amphitheatre, balancing this classical
structure with a Pictish salmon and a spiral. This was one of a
number of works commissioned by TSWA (TV South-West Arts)
throughout Britain in 1987. In Glasgow as part of this same
project George Wyllie produced an icon of socio-political insight
in *The Straw Locomotive* (1987), a sculptural event which was   165
both a reflection on the demise of heavy industry and a question- 166
ing of the nature of colonialism.

Admired by Wyllie was the German artist Joseph Beuys
(1921–86) whom he had met through the innovative Edinburgh
gallery director and artist Richard Demarco (b. 1930). At

163. **Will Maclean,** *Land Raid Memorial*, 1996. A combination of earthworks and stone construction at Gress, near Stornoway, this is one of three community-commissioned memorials on the Isle of Lewis. Each commemorates an episode in the struggle between crofters and landlords in the nineteenth and early twentieth centuries, echoing works such as McTaggart's emigrant ship paintings from a century before.

Demarco's invitation Beuys worked frequently in Scotland from the early 1970s until his death. Their joint commitment to art as an everyday experience which can unite spectacle, performance, philosophy and ecology received little establishment support but the spiritual, alchemical and ecological currents in Beuys' work struck a chord with a number of Scottish artists. Alchemy in particular has been a concern in the installations and paintings of Glen Onwin (b. 1947) and the paintings and prints of Ian Howard (b. 1952). In very different ways both of these artists have seen the thinking of the late-Renaissance period, during which alchemical thought reached its zenith, as crucial to the understanding of the present, whether in terms of the transformative nature of the earth and its ecology or the history of ideas. Symbolic of the growing interest in a more conceptual art and of the problems in supporting this in Scotland was the short-lived Ceramic Workshop in Edinburgh, which flourished from 1970 to 1974. During this time it was the venue for installations by, among others, Merilyn Smith (b. 1942) and the Romanian artist Paul Neagu. When forced to close, the workshop was transformed by its board

164. **Maud Sulter** *Clio*, 1989. The struggle for history and histories could not be clearer than in Sulter's work. Here Clio, the muse of history is given a new lease of life in which neither cultural imperialism nor the classical ideal can be taken for granted.

167. (opposite) **David Mach** *Big Heids*, 1999. The twenty foot high 'heids' were loosely modelled on three volunteers recruited within the North Lanarkshire area. Built up from thousands of welded steel sections, they echo the industrial history of the area.

165. (top) **George Wyllie** *The Burning of the Straw Locomotive, Glasgow, 10.30 pm, 22nd June, 1987*, 1987. Influenced by contact with Joseph Beuys, Wyllie's spectacular sculptural performances have linked popular accessibility and philosophical challenge. Here an icon of the lost past of heavy industry, recreated from a natural material, reveals a question mark in its ashes.

166. **George Wyllie** *The Straw Locomotive, 23rd June, 1987*, 1987.

168. (right) **Kate Whiteford** *Calton Hill Drawings*, 1987. Working on Calton Hill in the heart of Edinburgh, Kate Whiteford brought together Celtic and classical symbolism in a temporary installation of marble chips around the pillars of the National Monument. The image reproduced here is by the photographer Patricia Macdonald who has herself made a significant contribution to visual thinking in Scotland.

into a conceptual restatement of the uneasy relationship between art and money. £1512, the monetary realisation of the remaining assets of the workshop, was invested in an inaccessible account to accrue interest eternally. Cognate with the input of Beuys was that of the English artist John Latham (b. 1921), who worked in Scotland as a result of the enlightened patronage of the Scottish Office. Latham's Scottish work was centred on the monumental *Niddrie Woman* (1975), a redefinition of an entire post-industrial landscape of shale bings in West Lothian. Along with Beuys, Latham contributed to a current of ideas-based art which was developing in Scotland in the 1970s and 1980s, not least through the teaching of David Harding (b. 1937) who in 1985 was appointed to head the new Environmental Art Department at Glasgow School of Art. This contrasts with the situation in the 1960s, a decade during which most concept-inclined artists had gone to London, for example the performance artist and painter Bruce MacLean (b. 1944). London-based also was Mark Boyle (b. 1934) who, along with his partner Joan Hills, (b. 1936) had begun to challenge the nature of representation and objectivity. They did this by making replicas of randomly chosen ground sections in their project *Journey to the Surface of the Earth*, the first element of which was made in 1964. The change in atmosphere can be felt in the success of the ideas-based work of artists from the mid-1980s onwards, for example *Whaur Extremes Meet* (1989–90) a MacDiarmid-inspired, trans-European project developed by Wendy Gunn (b. 1963) and Gavin Renwick (b. 1964). Of particular significance from this period are those artists who developed their work in association with Transmission Gallery and *Variant* magazine in Glasgow, one of whom, Douglas Gordon (b. 1966), went on to win the Turner Prize in 1996 while another, Christine Borland (b. 1965), was short-listed the following year.

169. **Christine Borland** *Phantom Twins* (detail), 1997. Borland's work addresses issues of traces, remains and loss of identity, often via consideration of the techniques of forensic science and the history of medical teaching, the latter in this illustration. She is one of a group of artists, including Douglas Gordon, Craig Richardson and Ross Sinclair, associated with Glasgow's Transmission Gallery from the late 1980s onwards. All have explored the edges of accepted cultural knowledge in their work.

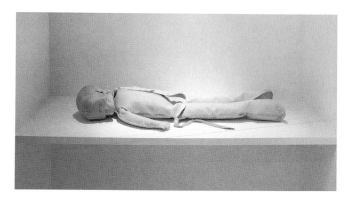

170. **Alan Johnston** *Installation shot,* exhibition in Haus Wittgenstein, Vienna, 1994. One of the most philosophically-aware artists of his generation, Johnston's paintings complement the subtleties of both Wittgenstein's architecture and his thinking.

The painter Callum Innes (b. 1962) had been short-listed for the Turner Prize in 1995. This gives some idea of the vitality and scope of Scottish art in the 1990s, for Innes's non-figurative paintings are very different in medium and intention from Douglas Gordon's word and video-based presentations, or Christine Borland's forensic investigations of the archaeology of knowledge. Innes is part of a lineage which leads back to William Johnstone's use of Eastern calligraphic techniques on the one hand and relates to American minimalism on the other. He was trained at Gray's School of Art in Aberdeen and subsequently at Edinburgh College of Art where Alan Johnston (b. 1945) was teaching. From the mid-1970s Johnston had developed a philosophically informed minimalism which resonated with the approach of Kenneth Dingwall (b. 1938), who also taught at Edinburgh before pursuing a successful career in America. One of Johnston's deepest influences has been Japanese art and philosophy, not least the paintings and garden designs of Sesshu (1420–1506). Other artists who share such interest in form, void and gestural subtlety include Ian McKenzie Smith (b. 1935), Eileen Lawrence (b. 1946) and London-based John McLean (b. 1939). Alan Johnston has balanced such factors with a commitment to Scottish philosophy, not least to David Hume's views on abstraction, which can be re-read as a kind of minimalist manifesto.

171

169

170

171. **Callum Innes**. *Untitled: Exposed Painting Cadmium Orange*, 1995. Innes' pared-down approach to painting, in which gravity plays a part in the movement of the paint, began to be widely appreciated in the mid-1990s.

172. (below) **Jack Knox** *Aftermath*, c. 1961. Early abstract works such as this painting were precursors for Knox of a thoughtful rapprochement with still life.

173. **Steven Campbell** *Painting in Defence of the Migrants*, 1993. One of a group of painters trained at Glasgow School of Art, Campbell was at the forefront of reinvigorating figurative art in Scotland in the 1980s.

Counterpointing the private inspiration that Hume's thinking has given to artists inclined to abstraction, the philosopher has been elevated to heroic public status by the neo-classical sculptor Alexander Stoddart (b. 1959) His seated, larger-than-life statue of Hume has been a presence at the beginning of the High Street in Edinburgh since late 1997. Stoddart trained at Glasgow School of Art at a time of resurgence of the figurative throughout European art. In painting, a straightforward approach to the figure had been maintained at Glasgow by Douglas Percy Bliss (1900–1984) and David Donaldson (1916–96). Subsequently Jack Knox (b. 1936) became head of painting in 1981, bringing an understanding of abstraction into an exploration of representation. Influential on Glasgow students from 1979 onwards was Alexander Moffat, a portrait painter, the Scottish cultural emphasis of whose work has always been informed by international influences, among them Max Beckmann and R. B. Kitaj. Moffat was influenced by personal contact with Hugh MacDiarmid and notable among his works have been portrayals of Scottish writers including, as well as MacDiarmid, the poets Sorley MacLean and Norman McCaig. Moffat steered a generation of Glasgow figurative painters which included Steven Campbell (b. 1953), Adrian

176

172

174

174. **Alexander Moffat**, *Poets' Pub*, 1980. Moffat's interest in literature led him to create this allegorical painting of writers gathered round the figure of Hugh MacDiarmid. On his right stands Norman MacCaig, behind him Sorley MacLean (at the back) and Iain Crichton Smith, and to his left George Mackay Brown, Sydney Goodsir Smith, Edwin Morgan and Robert Garioch. In the foreground is Alan Bold.

Wiszniewski (b. 1958), Peter Howson (b. 1958), Ken Currie (b. 1960), and Stephen Conroy (b. 1964). These painters became an identifiable Glasgow aspect of the New Image painting that was attracting so many artists both north and south of the Border during the early 1980s. Influences ranged from the Mexican mural-artist Diego Rivera (1886–1957) and the German Jorg Immendorff (b. 1945) in the political and societal preoccupations of Howson and Currie, to Degas in the lucid portraiture of Conroy. A debt is also owed to the figurative work of two Glasgow artists who are better known as writers, Alasdair

177

175. (right above) **Adrian Wiszniewski** *The Master Gardener*, 1988. Wiszniewski inclines to rhythmic, decorative classicism rather than social and political engagement.

176. (right below) **Alexander Stoddart** *Hume*, 1997. Hume is shown in heroic, classical mode, close to the High Kirk of St Giles and to the Advocates' Library of which he was librarian.

Gray (b. 1934) and John Byrne (b. 1940). Both Campbell and 178 Wiszniewski responded to the classical tradition, the latter as a kind of rococo Postmodernist, Campbell in a more critically- 175 engaged way, beginning to tackle issues of utopianism and 173 modernism with occasional echoes of Ian Hamilton Finlay on the one hand and Ruskin on the other. These Glasgow artists were to some extent paralleled in Edinburgh both by artists associated with the 369 Gallery, such as Caroline McNairn (b. 1955), and by slightly younger painters coming out of Edinburgh College of Art, for example Robert Maclaurin (b. 1961) and Gwen Hardie (b. 1962). Hardie went on to study with Georg Baselitz in Berlin

177. (left) **Stephen Conroy**
Sir Steven Runciman, 1990.
Conroy's painting of the eminent historian is a work of understated but powerful characterization. This modern portrait gains from the fact that the the artist draws deeply on the tradition of portraiture in Western art.

178. (above) **Alasdair Gray**
Jim Kelman, 1985. Alasdair Gray studied at Glasgow School of Art in the 1950s, and is well known as a novelist and designer/illustrator of his own books. Here he portrays his friend and fellow writer James Kelman.

179. **Ken Currie** *The Great Reform Agitation: Unity is Strength*, 1987. One of a series of murals depicting the radical history of Glasgow and commissioned for the People's Palace in that city. Currie brings both the influence of the comic strip and that of Diego Rivera to bear in his art.

and this experience added to her already powerful ability to articulate the female body both as representation and as symbol.

A theme that has run through this book is that of the interwoven fabric of verbal and visual art in Scotland. Examples can be found in the Book of Kells, the work of the two Allan Ramsays – poet and painter, father and son – or in the integration of word, form and image in the work of Ian Hamilton Finlay. One can see this link also in Jake Harvey's memorial in steel and bronze to Hugh MacDiarmid (1984) which evokes the poet's local, international and ecological vision. Harvey's work also touches on another theme of this book. He is one of a number of Scottish artists working at the time of writing who have responded to much earlier cultures in their work. In stone carvings from the 1990s he explored the cup and ring marks and carved stones of Scottish prehistory, giving the activities of those artists of 5000

182

180

181

180. **Jake Harvey** *Hugh MacDiarmid Memorial*, 1982–84. Sited near the poet's birthplace at Langholm, Harvey's sculpture in bronze and steel echoes not only poetry but also the land, reflecting the role that it plays in MacDiarmid's work.

years ago a reality which seems only a small psychological step from our present. I hope I have given due weight here both to such connections within the art of Scotland over time, and to the wider European context of which this art has always been part.

181. (above right) **Jake Harvey**
Cup Stones, 1993. A work that
makes a link across the millennia
to the cup and ring marks made
by the artists of prehistoric
Scotland.

182. (right) **Gwen Hardie** *Fist*,
1986. Hardie's radical re-thinking
of bodily form enabled her to
produce remarkable paintings
from the mid-1980s onwards.

Select Bibliography

General Works

Michael Apted & Susan Hannabuss, *Painters in Scotland 1301–1700: A Biographical Dictionary*, Edinburgh, 1978.

Robert Brydall, *Art in Scotland: Its Origin and Progress*, Edinburgh, 1889.

Jenni Calder (ed.), *The Wealth of a Nation*, Edinburgh, 1989.

Mungo Campbell, *The Line of Tradition: Watercolours, Drawings and Prints by Scottish Artists 1700–1990*, Edinburgh, 1993.

James L. Caw, *Scottish Painting: Past and Present, 1620–1908*, Edinburgh, 1908.

Stanley Cursiter, *Scottish Art to the Close of the Nineteenth Century*, London, 1949.

Lindsay Errington (ed.), *Scotland's Pictures*, Edinburgh, 1990.

Ian Finlay, *Scottish Art*, London, 1947.

Ian Finlay, *Scottish Crafts*, London, 1948.

I. F. Grant & Hugh Cheape, *Periods in Highland History*, London, 1987.

Julian Halsby, *Scottish Watercolours*, London, 1986.

William Hardie, *Scottish Painting 1837 to the Present*, London, 1990.

Paul Harris & Julian Halsby, *The Dictionary of Scottish Painters, 1600 to the Present*, Edinburgh, 1998.

Keith Hartley, *Scottish Art Since 1900*, Edinburgh, 1989.

James Holloway & Lindsay Errington, *The Discovery of Scotland*, Edinburgh, 1978.

James Holloway, *Patrons and Painters: Art in Scotland, 1650–1760*, Edinburgh, 1989.

David Irwin & Francina Irwin, *Scottish Painters at Home and Abroad 1700–1900*, London, 1975.

Wendy Kaplan (ed.), *Scotland Creates: 5000 Years of Art and Design*, London, 1990.

Michael Lynch, *A New History of Scotland*, London, 1991.

Peter McEwan, *Dictionary of Scottish Art and Architecture*, London, 1994.

William D. McKay, *The Scottish School of Painting*, London, 1906.

Duncan Macmillan, *Painting in Scotland: The Golden Age*, London, 1986.

Duncan Macmillan, *Scottish Art 1460–1990*, Edinburgh, 1990.

Duncan Macmillan, *Scottish Art in the Twentieth Century*, Edinburgh, 1994.

Fiona Pearson (ed.), *Virtue and Vision; Sculpture and Scotland 1540–1990*, Edinburgh, 1991.

Graham Ritchie & Anna Ritchie, *Scotland, Archaeology and Early History*, Edinburgh, 1991.

Paul H. Scott (ed.), *Scotland: A Concise Cultural History*, Edinburgh, 1993.

Sara Stevenson et al., *Light from the Dark Room: A Celebration of Scottish Photography*, Edinburgh, 1995.

John Tonge, *The Arts of Scotland*, London, 1938.

Andrew Gibbon Williams & Andrew Brown, *The Bigger Picture: A History of Scottish Art*, London, 1993. [Also a related set of BBC videos of the same title.]

Chapter One. Prehistory and Early History

Ian Armit, *Celtic Scotland*, London, 1997.

P. J. Ashmore, *Neolithic and Bronze Age Scotland*, London, 1996.

Richard Bradley, *Altering the Earth: The Origins of Monuments in Britain and Continental Europe*, Edinburgh, 1993.

Aubrey Burl, *The Stone Circles of the British Isles*, New Haven and London, 1976.

D. V. Clarke, T. G. Cowie, & A. Foxon (eds.), *Symbols of Power at the Time of Stonehenge*, Edinburgh, 1985.

Lawrence Keppie, *Scotland's Roman Remains*, Edinburgh, 1986.

Ruth Megaw & Vincent Megaw, *Celtic Art*, London, 1989.

Ronald W. B. Morris, *The Prehistoric Rock Art of Argyll*, Poole, 1977.

Wendy Doniger O'Flaherty (trans.), *The Rig Veda: an Anthology*, London, 1981.

T. G. E. Powell, *The Celts*, London, 1958.

Colin Renfrew, *Archaeology and Language: The Puzzle of Indo-European Origins*, London, 1987.

J. B. Stevenson, 'The Prehistoric Rock Carvings of Argyll', in Graham Ritchie (ed.), *The Archaeology of Argyll*, Edinburgh, 1998.

Archibald Thom, *Walking in All the Squares: A Biography of Alexander Thom, Engineer and Archaeoastronomer*, Glendaruel, 1995.

Chapter Two. The Development of Christian Art

Daphne Brooke, *Wild Men and Holy Places: St Ninian, Whithorn and the Medieval Realm of Galloway*, Edinburgh, 1994.

Brendan Cassidy (ed.), *The Ruthwell Cross*, Princeton, 1992.

Nora Chadwick, *Celtic Britain*, London, 1963.

Peter Berresford Ellis & Roy Ellsworth, *The Book of Deer*, London, 1994.

Ian Fisher, 'Early Christian Archaeology in Argyll', in G. Ritchie (ed.), *The Archaeology of Argyll*, Edinburgh, 1998.

Sally M. Foster, *Picts, Gaels and Scots*, London, 1996.

Sally M. Foster (ed.), *The St Andrews Sarcophagus: A Pictish Masterpiece and its International Connections*, Dublin, 1998.

George Henderson, *From Durrow to Kells: the Insular Gospel-Books 650–800*, London, 1987.

Isabel Henderson, *The Picts*, London, 1967.

Anthony Jackson, *The Symbol Stones of Scotland*, Kirkwall, 1984.

Lloyd Laing & Jennifer Laing, *Art of the Celts*, London, 1992.

Bernard Meehan, *The Book of Kells*, London, 1994.

Bernard Meehan, *The Book of Durrow*, Dublin, 1996.

Carl Nordenfalk, *Celtic and Anglo-Saxon Painting*, London, 1977.

Anna Ritchie, *Viking Scotland*, London, 1993.

Anna Ritchie, *Iona*, London, 1997.

R. Michael Spearman & John Higgitt (eds.), *The Age of Migrating Ideas: Early Medieval Art in Northern Britain and Ireland*, Edinburgh, 1993

Kenneth Steer, John Bannerman, & G. H. Collins, *Late Medieval Monumental Sculpture in the West Highlands*, Edinburgh, 1977.

Neil Stratford, *The Lewis Chessmen and the Enigma of the Hoard*, London, 1997.

Arnold Toynbee, *A Study of History*, abridged by D. C. Somerville, London, 1946, [esp. vol I: 155].

Chapter Three. Loss and Reconstruction

Michael Apted, *The Painted Ceilings of Scotland 1550–1650*, Edinburgh, 1966.

Alexander Broadie, *The Tradition of Scottish Philosophy*, Edinburgh, 1990.

David H. Caldwell (ed.), *Angels, Nobles and Unicorns: Art and Patronage in Medieval Scotland*, Edinburgh, 1982.

David H. Caldwell, 'In Search of Scottish Art: Native Traditions and Foreign Influences', in Wendy Kaplan (ed.), *Scotland Creates*, London, 1990.

George Henderson, 'The Seal of Brechin Cathedral', in Anne O'Connor & D. V. Clarke (eds.), *From the Stone Age to the 'Forty-Five*, Edinburgh, 1983.

John Higgitt, 'Art and the Church before the Reformation', in Wendy Kaplan (ed.), *Scotland Creates*, London, 1990.

David Howarth, 'Sculpture and Scotland 1540–1700', in Fiona Pearson (ed.), *Virtue and Vision; Sculpture and Scotland 1540–1990*, Edinburgh, 1991.

David McRoberts, 'The Fifteenth-Century Altarpiece of Fowlis Easter Church', in Anne O'Connor & D. V. Clarke (eds.), *From the Stone Age to the 'Forty-Five*, Edinburgh, 1983.

Rosalind K. Marshall, *John de Medina*, Edinburgh, 1988.

Thomas Ross, 'Ancient Sundials of Scotland', *Proceedings of the Society of Antiquaries of Scotland*, 21, 1889–90: 161–273.

Sara Stevenson, *John Michael Wright, the King's Painter*, Edinburgh, 1982.

Jeffrey Stone, *The Pont Manuscript Maps of Scotland: Sixteenth Century Origins of a Blaeu Atlas*, Tring, 1989.

Colin Thompson & Lorne Campbell, *Hugo van der Goes and the Trinity Panels in Edinburgh*, Edinburgh, 1974.

Duncan Thomson, *The Life and Work of George Jamesone*, Oxford, 1974.

Duncan Thomson, *Painting in Scotland 1570–1650*, Edinburgh, 1975.
Julia Lloyd Williams (ed.), *Dutch Art and Scotland: A Reflection of Taste*, Edinburgh, 1992.

Chapter Four. Classicism and Celticism
Iain Gordon Brown, *Poet & Painter: Allan Ramsay, Father and Son*, Edinburgh, 1984.
Lindsay Errington, 'Gavin Hamilton's Sentimental Iliad', *Burlington Magazine*, 120, January, 1978.
Howard Gaskill (ed.), *Ossian Revisited*, Edinburgh, 1991.
T. Crowther Gordon, *David Allan of Alloa: The Scottish Hogarth*, Alva, 1951.
Hanna Hohl & Hélène Toussaint, *Ossian*, catalogue of exhibition at Kunsthalle, Hamburg, and Grand Palais, Paris. Paris, 1974.
James Holloway, *James Tassie*, Edinburgh, 1986.
James Holloway, *Jacob More*, Edinburgh, 1987.
James Holloway, *William Aikman*, Edinburgh, 1988.
James Holloway, *The Norie Family*, Edinburgh, 1994.
Serena Q. Hutton, '"A Historical Painter": Gavin Hamilton in 1755', *Burlington Magazine*, 120, January, 1978: 25–27.
David Irwin, 'Gavin Hamilton: Archaeologist, Painter and Dealer', *Art Bulletin*, 44, no. 2, 1962: 87–108.
David Irwin, *Neoclassicism*, London, 1997.
Raymond Lister, *British Romantic Painting*, Cambridge, 1989.
Murdo Macdonald, 'The Torrent Shrieks: James Macpherson and Scottish Culture', in R. A. Jamieson (ed.), *Edinburgh Review*, 96, 1996.
Duncan Macmillan, 'Alexander Runciman in Rome', *Burlington Magazine*, 112, Jan. 1970: 22–31.
Duncan Macmillan, 'Truly National Designs; Runciman at Penicuik', *Art History*, 1, 1978: 90–98.
Duncan Macmillan, 'Old and Plain: Music and Song in Scottish Art', in Edward J. Cowan (ed.), *The People's Past*, Edinburgh, 1980.
Thomas Markus (ed.), *Order in Space and Society: Architectural Form and its Context in the Scottish Enlightenment*, Edinburgh, 1982.
Robert Rosenblum, 'The Origin of Painting: A Problem in the Iconography of Romantic Classicism', *Art Bulletin*, 39, Dec. 1957: 279–90.
Robert Rosenblum, 'Gavin Hamilton's Brutus and its Aftermath', *Burlington Magazine*, 103, January, 1961: 8–16.
Robert Rosenblum, 'A Source for David's "Horatii"', *Burlington Magazine*, 112, May 1970: 269–73.
Alastair Smart, *Allan Ramsay*, New Haven and London, 1992.
Margaret H. B. Sanderson, *Robert Adam and Scotland*, Edinburgh, 1992

Werner Spies, 'The Nordic Homer and Romanticism: "Ossian" – an exhibition at the Louvre and Kunsthalle Hamburg 1974', reprinted in Werner Spies, *Focus on Art*, New York, 1982.
Julia Lloyd Williams, *Gavin Hamilton*, Edinburgh, 1994.

Chapter Five. Painting and Philosophy
Linda Colley, *Britons*, New Haven and London, 1992, [esp. 'Conclusion'].
William J. Chiego, H. A. D. Miles, David B. Brown, *Sir David Wilkie of Scotland*, Raleigh, North Carolina, 1987.
J. C. B. Cooksey, *Alexander Nasmyth, 1758–1840*, Whittinghame, 1991.
George Davie, *The Democratic Intellect*, Edinburgh, 1961, [esp. ch. 7, 'Geometry or Algebra'].
Lindsay Errington, *Tribute to Wilkie*, Edinburgh, 1985.
Lindsay Errington, *Alexander Carse*, Edinburgh, 1987.
Terry Friedman, 'Samuel Joseph and the Sculpture of Feeling', in Fiona Pearson (ed.), *Virtue and Vision; Sculpture and Scotland 1540–1990*, Edinburgh, 1991.
Ésme Gordon, *The Royal Scottish Academy of Painting, Sculpture and Architecture 1826–1976*, Edinburgh, 1976.
Julie Lawson, 'The Painter's Vision' in Julie Lawson, Sara Stevenson and Heinz & Bridget Henisch, *Visions of the Ottoman Empire*, Edinburgh, 1994.
Stephen Lloyd, *Raeburn's Rival: Archibald Skirving 1749–1819*, Edinburgh, 1999.
Duncan Macmillan, 'Géricault et Charles Bell' in *Géricault*, Tome I, Louvre conferences et colloques, Paris, 1996: 452–91
Helen Smailes, *John Zephaniah Bell*, Edinburgh, 1990.
Helen Smailes, 'Thomas Campbell and Lawrence Macdonald: the Roman Solution to the Scottish Sculptor's Dilemma', in Fiona Pearson (ed.), *Virtue and Vision; Sculpture and Scotland 1540–1990*, Edinburgh, 1991.
Duncan Thomson, *Raeburn*, Edinburgh, 1997, [with contributions from John Dick, David Mackie and Nicholas Phillipson].

Chapter Six. Nineteenth-Century Narratives
M. H. Noel-Paton & J. P. Campbell, *Joseph Noel Paton 1821–1901*, Edinburgh, 1990.
Walter Benjamin, 'A Small History of Photography' (1931), in Walter Benjamin (ed. Susan Sontag), *One Way Street*, New York, 1978.
Mungo Campbell, *David Scott*, Edinburgh, 1990.
James L. Caw, *William McTaggart, a Biography and an Appreciation*, Glasgow, 1917.
Lindsay Errington, *Masterclass: Robert Scott Lauder and his Pupils*, Edinburgh, 1983.
Lindsay Errington, *Robert Herdman*, Edinburgh, 1988.

Lindsay Errington, *William McTaggart*, Edinburgh, 1989.
Lindsay Errington, 'Sir Walter Scott and Nineteenth-Century Painting in Scotland', in Wendy Kaplan (ed.), *Scotland Creates*, London, 1990.
Gerald Finley, *Landscapes of Memory: Turner as Illustrator to Scott*, London, 1980.
Helen Guiterman, *David Roberts RA*, London, 1978.
Martin Hardie, *John Pettie*, London, 1908
Hilda Orchardson Gray, *The Life of Sir William Quiller Orchardson*, London, 1930.
Elspeth King, Introduction to William Hamilton of Gilbertfield's adaptation of *Blind Harry's Wallace*, Edinburgh, 1997.
Georg Lukacs, *The Historical Novel*, London, 1962.
Mary McKerrow, *The Faeds*, Edinburgh, 1982.
Fiona Pearson, 'Sir John Steell and the Idea of a Native School of Sculpture', in Fiona Pearson (ed.), *Virtue and Vision; Sculpture and Scotland 1540–1990*, Edinburgh, 1991.
Edward Pinnington, *G. P. Chalmers and the Art of his Time*, Glasgow, 1896.
Marcia Pointon, *William Dyce, 1806–1864: A Critical Biography*, Oxford, 1979.
Dante Gabriel Rossetti, supplementary chapter to Alexander Gilchrist, *The Life of William Blake*, London, 1863.
William Bell Scott, *Memoir of David Scott RSA*, Edinburgh, 1850.
Helen Smailes, *A Portrait Gallery for Scotland*, Edinburgh, 1985.
Helen Smailes & Duncan Thomson, *The Queen's Image: A Celebration of Mary, Queen of Scots*, Edinburgh, 1987.
Sheena Smith, *Horatio McCulloch*, Glasgow, 1988.
Sara Stevenson, *Hill and Adamson's 'The Fishermen and Women of the Firth of Forth'*, Edinburgh, National Galleries of Scotland, 1991.
Robin Lee Woodward, 'Pittendrigh Macgillivray' in Fiona Pearson (ed.), *Virtue and Vision; Sculpture and Scotland 1540–1990*, Edinburgh, 1991.

Chapter Seven. Modernity and Revivals
Philip Athill (ed.), *William Strang*, Sheffield, 1981.
Roger Billcliffe, *The Glasgow Boys: The Glasgow School of Painting 1875–1895*, London, 1985.
David Brett, *C. R. Mackintosh: The Poetics of Workmanship*, London, 1992.
Gordon H. Brown & Hamish Keith, *New Zealand Painting*, Auckland, 1969, [esp. ch. 6, 'James McLachlan Nairn'].
Nicola Gordon Bowe & Elizabeth Cumming, *The Arts and Crafts Movements in Dublin and Edinburgh*, Dublin, 1998.
William Buchanan, *The Art of the Photographer J. Craig Annan*, Edinburgh, 1992.

Jude Burkhauser (ed.), *'Glasgow Girls': Women in Art and Design 1880–1920*, Edinburgh, 1990.

James L. Caw, *Sir James Guthrie*, London, 1932.

Alan Crawford, *Charles Rennie Mackintosh*, London, 1995.

Elizabeth Cumming, 'A Gleam of Renaissance Hope: Edinburgh at the Turn of the Century', in Wendy Kaplan (ed.), *Scotland Creates*, London, 1990.

Elizabeth Cumming, *Phoebe Anna Traquair*, Edinburgh, 1993.

Elizabeth Cumming, *Glasgow 1900*, Amsterdam, 1993.

Michael Donnelly, *Scotland's Stained Glass*, Edinburgh, 1997.

Iain Gale, *Melville*, Edinburgh, 1996.

Vivien Hamilton, *Joseph Crawhall*, London, 1990.

William Hardie, 'George Dutch Davidson', *Scottish Art Review*, vol. 13, no. 4, 1972: 18–23.

Janice Helland, *The Studios of Frances and Margaret Macdonald*, Manchester, 1996.

Thomas Howarth, *Charles Rennie Mackintosh and the Modern Movement*, London, 1952.

Wendy Kaplan (ed.), *Charles Rennie Mackintosh*, London, 1996.

John Kemplay, *John Duncan: A Scottish Symbolist*, San Francisco, 1994.

A. P. Lawrie, *The Painter's Methods and Materials*, London, 1926.

E. S. Lumsden, *The Art of Etching*, London, 1924.

Kenneth McConkey, *Sir John Lavery*, Edinburgh, 1993.

Jennifer Melville, *Pittendrigh Macgillivray*, Aberdeen, 1988.

Jennifer Melville, *Robert Brough*, Aberdeen, 1995.

Timothy Neat, *Part Seen, Part Imagined: Meaning and Symbolism in the Work of Charles Rennie Mackintosh and Margaret Macdonald*, Edinburgh, 1994.

Pamela Robertson, *Charles Rennie Mackintosh: Art is the Flower*, London, 1995.

John Ruskin, 'Of Leaf Beauty', *Modern Painters*, Part VI, London, 1860.

Tomoko Sato & Toshio Watanabe, *Japan and Britain: An Aesthetic Dialogue 1850–1930*, London, 1991.

Ann Simpson (ed.), *James Pryde*, Edinburgh, 1992.

Bill Smith, *D. Y. Cameron*, Edinburgh, 1992.

Bill Smith, *Hornel*, Edinburgh, 1997.

Paul Stirton, 'Grez-sur-Loing, an artists' colony', *Journal of the Scottish Society for Art History*, 1, 1996: 40–53.

Ailsa Tanner, *Bessie MacNicol*, privately published, 1998.

Peter Vergo, *Vienna 1900: Vienna, Scotland and the European Avant-Garde*, Edinburgh, 1983.

Colin White, *The Enchanted World of Jessie M. King*, Edinburgh, 1989.

Claire A. P. Willsdon, 'Paul Serusier the

Celt: did he paint murals in Edinburgh?', *The Burlington Magazine*, 126, 1984: 88–91.

Chapter Eight. Twentieth-Century Pluralism

Yves Abrioux, *Ian Hamilton Finlay: A Visual Primer*, 2nd edition, London, 1992.

Patrick Bourne, *Anne Redpath*, Edinburgh, 1989.

Roger Billcliffe, *The Scottish Colourists: Cadell, Fergusson, Hunter and Peploe*, London, 1989.

Elizabeth Cumming et al., *Colour Rhythm and Dance: Paintings and Drawings by J. D. Fergusson and his Circle in Paris*, Edinburgh, 1985.

Stanley Cursiter Centenary Exhibition, Pier Art Gallery, Stromness, 1987.

Alan Davie (ed.), *Alan Davie*, with essays by Douglas Hall and William Tucker, London, 1992.

Patrick Elliott, *William McCance*, Edinburgh, 1990.

Patrick Elliott, *Edward Baird*, Edinburgh, 1992.

Alec Finlay (ed.), *Wood Notes Wild: Essays on Ian Hamilton Finlay*, Edinburgh, 1995.

Edward Gage, *The Eye in the Wind: Contemporary Scottish Painting Since 1945*, London, 1997.

Iain Gale, *William MacTaggart 1903–1981*, Edinburgh, 1998.

William Gear and COBRA, exhibition catalogue, Aberdeen Art Gallery, Aberdeen, 1998.

Ian Gow, 'The Scottish National War Memorial', in Fiona Pearson (ed.), *Virtue and Vision; Sculpture and Scotland 1540–1990*, Edinburgh, 1991.

Douglas Hall, *William Johnstone*, Edinburgh, 1980.

Douglas Hall, 'The Twentieth Century', in Fiona Pearson (ed.), *Virtue and Vision; Sculpture and Scotland 1540–1990*, Edinburgh, 1991.

Bill Hare, *Contemporary Painting in Scotland*, Sydney, 1992.

Keith Hartley, Clare Henry et al., *The Vigorous Imagination: New Scottish Art*, Scottish National Gallery of Modern Art, Edinburgh, 1987.

Adrian Henri, *Environments and Happenings*, London, 1974. [For commentary on Joseph Beuys' work in Scotland, Mark Boyle's early London work, etc.]

Tom Hewlett, *Cadell: The Life and Works of a Scottish Colourist*, London, 1988.

John Kemplay, *The Two Companions: The Story of Two Scottish Artists, Eric Robertson and Cecile Walton*, Edinburgh, 1991.

John Kemplay, *The Edinburgh Group*, exhibition catalogue, City Art Centre, Edinburgh, 1983

Philip Long, *William Gillies: Watercolours of Scotland*, Edinburgh, 1994.

Philip Long, *John Maxwell*, Edinburgh, 1998.

Philip Long, *Anne Redpath*, Edinburgh, 1996.

John McEwen & Tamara Krikorian, 'William Johnstone: A Survey', *Studio International*, vol. 189, no. 974, March/April 1975: 88–92.

John McEwan, *John Bellany*, Edinburgh 1994.

David McLure, *John Maxwell*, Edinburgh, 1976.

Duncan Macmillan, *Symbols of Survival: The Art of Will Maclean*, Edinburgh, 1992.

Duncan Macmillan, *Jake Harvey*, Edinburgh, 1993.

Margaret Morris, *The Art of J. D. Fergusson*, Glasgow, 1974.

New Image Glasgow, Third Eye Centre, Glasgow, 1985.

Tom Normand, 'Scottish Modernism and Scottish Identity', in Wendy Kaplan (ed.), *Scotland Creates*, London, 1990.

Cordelia Oliver, *Joan Eardley, RSA*, Edinburgh, 1988.

Cordelia Oliver, *James Cowie*, Edinburgh, 1980.

Eduardo Paolozzi, *Eduardo Paolozzi: Recurring Themes*, Edinburgh, 1984.

Andrew Patrizio, *Contemporary Sculpture in Scotland*, Sydney, 1999.

Fiona Pearson, *William Wilson*, Edinburgh, 1994.

Scatter: New Scottish Art, Third Eye Centre, Glasgow, 1989.

Benno Schotz, *Bronze in My Blood*, Edinburgh, 1981.

Self Conscious State, Third Eye Centre, Glasgow, 1990.

Ann Simpson (ed.), *William Crozier*, Edinburgh, 1995.

W. Gordon Smith, *Robin Philipson*, Edinburgh, 1995.

Joanna Soden & Victoria Keller, *William Gillies*, Edinburgh, 1998.

William Turnbull: Sculpture and Paintings, Serpentine Gallery, London, 1996.

Lawrence Weaver, *The Scottish National War Memorial*, London, 1927.

Anne Wishart (ed.), *The Society of Scottish Artists: The First 100 Years*, Edinburgh, 1991.

George Wyllie, *Sculpture Jubilee*, Glasgow, 1991.

List of Illustrations

Dimensions are in centimetres, followed by inches, height before width before depth (where applicable)

Dimensions of symbol stones and cross slabs are approximate

Abbreviations:
NGS = National Gallery of Scotland, Edinburgh
SNPG = Scottish National Portrait Gallery, Edinburgh
SNGMA = Scottish National Gallery of Modern Art, Edinburgh

Frontispiece. William McTaggart, *The Storm*, 1890. Oil on canvas 121.9 x 183 (48 x 72). NGS
1. Standing Stones, Calanais, Isle of Lewis, Hebrides, *c.* 3000 BC. Photo: Edwin Smith
2. Elaborately decorated stone, probably a lintel from a cambered cairn, found at Pierowall, Westray, Orkney, *c.* 3000 BC. Tankerness House, Kirkwall, Orkney. Crown Copyright: Reproduced by Permission of Historic Scotland
3. Carved stone ball from Towie, Aberdeenshire, *c.* 2500 BC. © The Trustees of the National Museums of Scotland 2000
4. Cup and ring markings at Achnabreck, Argyll, *c.* 3500–2000 BC. Dimensions: 400 x 550 (157 ½ x 216 ½). Crown Copyright: Royal Commission on the Ancient and Historical Monuments of Scotland
5. Battle-axes from Broomend of Crichie, Aberdeenshire and Lochniddry, East Lothian, 2000–1500 BC. © The Trustees of the National Museums of Scotland 2000
6. Pony-cap from Torrs, Kirkcudbrightshire, 3rd century BC. © The Trustees of the National Museums of Scotland 2000
7. Carnyx (war trumpet), bronze, from Deskford, Banffshire, 1st century. © The Trustees of the National Museums of Scotland 2000
8. Roman sculpture of a lioness eating her prey (pulled from the mud of the River Almond at Cramond, Edinburgh in 1997), 2nd or 3rd century. © The Trustees of the National Museums of Scotland 2000 and with thanks to the City of Edinburgh Council
9. Sculpture of Brigantia from Birrens, Dumfriesshire, early 3rd century. © The Trustees of the National Museums of Scotland 2000
10. Front of cross slab, Glamis, Angus, 8th century. Red sandstone 266.7 x 167.6 at base and 142.2 at top (105 x 66 at base and 56 at top). Crown Copyright: Reproduced by Permission of Historic Scotland
11. Papil Stone, Burra, Shetland, 7th/8th century. Red sandstone, 208.3 x 47 x 5.1 (82 x 18 ½ x 2). Crown Copyright: Reproduced by Permission of Historic Scotland
12. Pictish symbol stone, Aberlemno, Angus, 6th/7th century. 180 x 90 x 20 (70 ⅞ x 35 ½ x 7 ⅞). Crown Copyright: Royal Commission on the Ancient and Historical Monuments of Scotland
13. Burghead bull, Morayshire, 7th century AD. Stylized bull carved on a stone slab, height 53 (20 ⅞). © The Trustees of the British Museum, London (MLA 1861.10-24.1)
14. Pictish cross slab, east face, Aberlemno churchyard, Angus, early 8th century. 230 high x 130 wide at the base, tapering to 90 at the top x 20 (90 ½ x 51 ⅛ tapering to 35 ½ x 7 ⅞). Crown Copyright: Royal Commission on the Ancient and Historical Monuments of Scotland
15. Biblical scene from surviving side panel of sarcophagus from St Andrews, Fife, probably late 8th century. Sandstone 64 x 108 x 10 (25 ¼ x 42 ½ x 4). Crown Copyright: Reproduced by Permission of Historic Scotland
16. Mary Magdalen washing the feet of Christ. Detail of stone cross from Ruthwell, Dumfriesshire, early 8th century. Photo Conway Library, Courtauld Institute, London
17. Carpet page from the Book of Durrow, Folio 3v. Probably made in Iona in the late 7th century. Photo courtesy of the Board of Trinity College, Dublin
18. St Martin's Cross, east face, St Mary's Abbey, Iona, 8th century. Height 403 (168). Crown Copyright: Royal Commission on the Ancient and Historical Monuments of Scotland
19. Kildalton Cross, north east face, Kildalton, Islay, 8th century. Height 265 (102). Crown Copyright: Royal Commission on the Ancient and Historical Monuments of Scotland
20. King no. 2 from the collection of 12th-century chess pieces found at Uig, Isle of Lewis. © The Trustees of the British Museum (Iv. Cat. 79)
21. Book of Kells, John I, I: *In Principio erat verbum* (In the beginning there was the word). Folio 292r, Iona, *c.* 800. Photo courtesy of the Board of Trinity College, Dublin
22. Grave slab of Murchadus MacDuffie of Colonsay, 1539. Carved stone, 170 x 48 (67 x 18 ⅞). Oronsay School, Oronsay Priory. Crown Copyright: Royal Commission on the Ancient and Historical Monuments of Scotland
23. Grave slab of Prioress Anna MacLean, 1543. St Mary's Abbey, Iona Nunnery. 213 x 66 (83 ⅞ x 26). Crown Copyright: Royal Commission on the Ancient and Historical Monuments of Scotland
24. *Annunciation* from the Beaton Panels, 1524–37. Wood carving. © The Trustees of the National Museums of Scotland 2000
25. Initial showing David I and Malcolm IV from a Charter of Malcolm IV to Kelso Abbey, 1159 or shortly after. Vellum, approx. size of overall charter 56.3 x 45 (22 ⅛ x 17 ¾). Duke of Roxburghe on deposit at the National Library of Scotland, Edinburgh
26. Anon., *The Crucifixion*, second half of the 15th century. Panel 160 x 401.4 (63 x 158). The Church of Fowlis Easter, Dundee. Crown Copyright: Reproduced by Permission of Historic Scotland
27. Seal of the Chapter of Brechin Cathedral (matrix), 13th century. Brass front (image of the Holy Trinity) 6 x 3.7 (2 ⅜ x 1 ½). © The Trustees of the National Museums of Scotland 2000
28. Arnold Bronckhorst (attrib.), *George Buchanan*, 1581. Oil on panel 34.1 x 27.7 (13 ½ x 11). SNPG
29. Adrian Vanson, *James VI of Scotland, later James I of England*, 1595. Oil on panel 72.9 x 62.3 (28 ⅝ x 24 ½). SNPG
30. George Jamesone, *Self-portrait*, 1637–40. Oil on canvas 68.5 x 83.8 (27 x 33). SNPG
31. *The Muses and Virtues*, *c.* 1599. Painted ceiling, Crathes Castle, Kincardineshire. Reproduced by kind permission of the National Trust for Scotland
32. John Michael Wright, *Sir William Bruce*, 1664. Oil on canvas 72.4 x 61 (28½ x 24). SNPG
33. John Michael Wright, *Lord Mungo Murray*, *c.* 1680. Oil on canvas 224.8 x 154.3 (88 ½ x 60 ¾). SNPG
34. Thomas Warrender, *Allegorical Still Life*, 1708. Oil on canvas 59.1 x 74.3 (23 ¼ x 29 ¼). NGS
35. James Norie, with additions by Jan Griffier II, *Taymouth Castle (from the south)*, 1733 (repainted 1739). Oil on canvas 66 x 133 (26 x 52 ⅜). SNPG
36. Jacob More, *The Falls of Clyde: Cora Linn*, 1771. Oil on canvas 79.4 x 100.4 (31 ¼ x 39 ½). NGS
37. William Aikman, *Self-portrait*, n.d. (possibly *c.* 1712). Oil on canvas 75.9 x 63 (29 ⅞ x 24 ⅞). SNPG
38. Richard Waitt, *Nic Ciarain, The Hen-wife of Castle Grant*, 1726. Oil on canvas 76.2 x 63.5 (30 x 25). Private Collection
39. John Alexander, *Lord Provost George Drummond*, 1752. Oil on canvas 124 x 101 (48 ⅞ x 39 ¾). Collection Edinburgh Royal Infirmary. © Medical Photography, Edinburgh Royal Infirmary

40. William Mosman, *John Campbell of the Bank*, 1749. Oil on canvas 145 x 118 (46 ½ x 57). Reproduced by kind permission of The Royal Bank of Scotland plc
41. Allan Ramsay, *Anne Bayne*, *c.* 1740. Oil on canvas 68.6 x 53.3 (27 x 21). SNPG
42. Allan Ramsay, *Hew Dalrymple, Lord Drummore*, 1754. Oil on canvas 127.6 x 99.7 (50 ¼ x 39 ¼). SNPG
43. Allan Ramsay, *Margaret Lindsay*, *c.* 1760. Oil on canvas 76.2 x 63.5 (30 x 25). NGS
44. Allan Ramsay, *David Hume*, 1766. Oil on canvas 76.2 x 63.5 (30 x 25). SNPG
45. Allan Ramsay, *Jean-Jacques Rousseau*, 1766. Oil on canvas 75.6 x 61.9 (29 ¾ x 24 ⅜). NGS
46. Gavin Hamilton, *Achilles Lamenting the Death of Patroclus*, 1760–63. Oil on canvas 227.3 x 391.2 (99 ½ x 154). NGS
47. David Allan, *Jenny and Roger*, from Allan Ramsay's *The Gentle Shepherd*, printed by A. Foulis, Glasgow, 1788. Aquatint 26.7 x 20.7 (10 x 8 ⅛). Dundee University Library
48. James Tassie, *Robert Adam*, 1792. Glass paste, height 7.8 (3 ⅛). SNPG
49. John Kay, *Self-portrait*, 1786. Etching 11.1 x 9.8 (4 ⅜ x 3 ⅞). SNPG
50. David Allan, *The Origin of Painting*, 1775. Oil on panel 38.1 x 30.5 (15 x 12). NGS
51. Alexander Runciman, *The Blind Ossian Singing and Accompanying Himself on the Harp*, sketch for the central part of the ceiling of the *Hall of Ossian*, 1772. Pen, brown wash and oil, oval 46.7 x 59.9 (18 ⅜ x 23 ½). NGS
52. John Runciman, *King Lear in the Storm*, 1767. Oil on panel 44.5 x 61 (17 ½ x 24). NGS
53. Alexander Runciman, *Fingal and Conban-cârgla*, *c.*1772. Etching 15 x 24.6 (5 ⅞ x 9 ⅝). Private Collection
54. Henry Raeburn, *Niel Gow*, *c.* 1793. Oil on canvas 123.2 x 97.8 (48 ½ x 38 ½). SNPG
55. Henry Raeburn, *Sir John and Lady Clerk of Penicuik*, 1791–92. Oil on canvas 145 x 206 (57 x 81). National Gallery of Ireland, Dublin
56. Henry Raeburn, *Isabella McLeod, Mrs James Gregory*, 1798. Oil on canvas 127 x 101.6 (50 x 40). Reproduced by kind permission of the National Trust for Scotland
57. Henry Raeburn, *Thomas Reid*, 1796. Oil on canvas 75.7 x 63.5 (29 ¾ x 25). Fyvie Castle Collection, Aberdeenshire. Reproduced by kind permission of the National Trust for Scotland
58. Henry Raeburn, *Colonel Alasdair Macdonell of Glengarry*, 1811. Oil on canvas 241.3 x 149.9 (95 x 59). NGS
59. Alexander Nasmyth, *Castle Huntly and the Tay*, *c.* 1800. Oil on canvas 114.9 x 170.8 (45 ¼ x 67 ¼). Dundee Arts & Heritage, McManus Galleries
60. Alexander Nasmyth, *Robert Burns*, 1787. Oil on canvas, oval, 38.4 x 32.4 (15 ⅛ x 12 ¾). SNPG
61. Alexander Nasmyth, *Edinburgh from Princes Street with the Commencement of the Building of the Royal Institution*, 1825. Oil on canvas 119.4 x 160 (47 x 63). NGS
62. John Knox, *Landscape with Tourists at Loch Katrine*, *c.* 1820. Oil on canvas 90 x 125 (35 ¾ x 49 ¼). NGS
63. David Wilkie, *William Chalmers Bethune, his wife Isobel Morison and their Daughter Isabella*, 1804. Oil on canvas 124.5 x 101.6 (49 x 40). NGS
64. David Wilkie, *Distraining for Rent*, 1815. Oil on panel 81.3 x 123 (32 x 48 ½). NGS
65. David Wilkie, *The Preaching of Knox Before the Lords of the Congregation, 10 July, 1559* (sketch), 1822. Oil on panel 49.5 x 62.2 (19 ½ x 24 ½). Petworth House, West Sussex. Photo: The National Trust Photographic Library
66. David Wilkie, *The Blind Fiddler*, 1806. Oil on panel 57.8 x 79.4 (22 ¾ x 31 ¼). © Tate Gallery, London 1999
67. Lawrence Macdonald, *George Combe*, *c.* 1830. Marble, height 69.4 (27 ⅜). SNPG
68. William Allan, *The Slave Market, Constantinople*, 1838. Oil on panel 129 x 198 (50 ¾ x 78). NGS
69. David Roberts, *Thebes, Karnac*, 1838. Watercolour and bodycolour 48.3 x 32.4 (19 x 12 ¾). Manchester City Art Galleries
70. John Thomson of Duddingston, *Fast Castle from Below*, *c.* 1824. Oil on canvas 76.2 x 105.4 (30 x 41 ½). NGS
71. Thomas Duncan, *The Death of John Brown of Priesthill*, 1844. Oil on canvas 132.1 x 208.3 (52 x 82). Glasgow Museums: Art Gallery & Museum, Kelvingrove
72. Robert Scott Lauder, *Christ Teacheth Humility*, 1847. Oil on canvas 233.7 x 353.1 (92 x 139). NGS
73. William Dyce, *Christ as the Man of Sorrows*, 1860. Oil on board 34.9 x 48.4 (13 ¾ x 19). NGS
74. David Octavius Hill and Robert Adamson, *Mrs Elizabeth (Johnstone) Hall*, *c.* 1844. Calotype 20.8 x 15.7 (8 ⅛ x 6 ⅛). SNPG
75. David Octavius Hill, *A View of Edinburgh from North of the Castle Rock, showing the Castle, the New Town, and the Firth of Forth*, 1859 or after. Oil on panel 81 x 155 (32 x 61). Reproduced by kind permission of The Royal Bank of Scotland plc
76. Horatio McCulloch, *Glencoe*, 1864. Oil on canvas 110.5 x 182.9 (43 ½ x 72). Glasgow Museums: Art Gallery & Museum, Kelvingrove
77. Thomas Faed, *The Last of the Clan*, 1865. Oil on canvas 144.8 x 182.9 (57 x 72). Glasgow Museums: Art Gallery & Museum, Kelvingrove
78 David Scott, *Puck Fleeing the Dawn*, 1837. Oil on canvas 95.2 x 146 (37 ½ x 57 ½). NGS
79 David Scott, *Philoctetes left in the island of Lemnos by the Greeks on their passage towards Troy*, 1839. Oil on canvas 90 x 125 (39 ¾ x 47). NGS
80 William Bell Scott, *In the Nineteenth Century the Northumbrians show the World what can be done with IRON and COAL*, 1855–60. Oil on canvas 185.4 x 185.4 (73 x 73). National Trust, Wallington Hall
81. James Drummond, *The Porteous Mob*, 1855. Oil on canvas 112 x 143 (44 x 60). NGS
82. Sir Joseph Noel Paton, *Dawn: Luther at Erfurt*, 1861. Oil on canvas 92.7 x 69 (36 ½ x 27 ⅛). NGS
83. Amelia Hill, *David Octavius Hill*, 1868. Marble, height 81 (31 ⅞). SNPG
84. William Fettes Douglas, *The Spell*, 1864. Oil on canvas 77.5 x 156.8 (30 ½ x 61 ¾). NGS
85. Robert Scott Lauder, *John Gibson Lockhart and his wife Charlotte Sophia Scott*, *c.* 1840. Oil on canvas 31.1 x 56.5 (12 ¾ x 22 ¼). SNPG
86. John Pettie, *Disbanded*, 1877. Oil on canvas 94.5 x 67.3 (37 ¼ x 26 ½). Dundee Arts & Heritage, McManus Galleries
87. Peter Graham, *Wandering Shadows*, 1878. Oil on canvas 134.6 x 182.8 (53 x 72). NGS
88. Sir William Quiller Orchardson, *Voltaire*, 1883. Oil on canvas 201.7 x 147.2 (79 ½ x 58). NGS
89. George Paul Chalmers, *The Legend*, 1864–78. Oil on canvas 101.6 x 150.5 (40 x 59 ¼). NGS
90. Robert Herdman, *After the Battle: A Scene in Covenanting Times*, 1870. Oil on canvas 115.9 x 172.7 (45 ⅝ x 68). NGS
91. Hugh Cameron, *A Lonely Life*, 1873. Oil on canvas 84.5 x 63.5 (33 ¼ x 25). NGS
92. George Reid, *Evening*, 1873. Oil on canvas 41.9 x 68.6 (16 ½ x 27). Dundee Arts and Heritage, McManus Galleries (Orchar Collection)
93. William McTaggart, *The Sailing of the Emigrant Ship*, 1895. Oil on canvas 75.6 x 86.4 (29 ¾ x 34). Glasgow Art Gallery and Museum
94. William McTaggart, *The Coming of St Columba*, 1895. Oil on canvas 131 x 206 (51 ½ x 81 ⅛). NGS
95. John Steell, *Sir Walter Scott*, detail from the Scott Monument, Princes Street, Edinburgh, 1840–46. Crown Copyright: Royal Commission on the Ancient and Historical Monuments of Scotland
96. D. W. Stevenson, *William Wallace*, 1887, from the National Wallace Monument, Stirling. Photo: The Argyll, the Isles, Loch Lomond, Stirling & Trossachs Tourist Board
97. Pittendrigh Macgillivray, *Robert Burns*, 1895. Maquette for the Burns Monument, Irvine. City of Aberdeen Art Gallery & Museums Collection
98. William Hole, *Processional Frieze*, 1898–1901 (detail). Mural on stone at SNPG
99. John Lavery, *The Tennis Party*, 1885. Oil on canvas 77 x 183.5 (30 ⅜ x 72 ¼). City of Aberdeen Art Gallery and Museums Collections. By courtesy of Felix Rosenstiel's Widow and Son Ltd., London on behalf of the Estate of Sir John Lavery

100. William York Macgregor, *The Vegetable Stall*, 1883–84. Oil on canvas 105.5 x 150.5 (41 ½ x 59 ½). NGS
101. James Guthrie, *A Hind's Daughter*, 1883. Oil on canvas 91.5 x 76.2 (36 x 30). NGS
102. Edward Arthur Walton, *A Berwickshire Fieldworker*, 1884. Oil on canvas 91.4 x 61.9 (36 x 24 ⅜). © Tate Gallery, London 1999
103. Bessie MacNicol, *A Girl of the 'Sixties'*, 1899. Oil on canvas 81.3 x 61 (32 x 24). Glasgow Museums: Art Gallery & Museum, Kelvingrove
104. Arthur Melville, *Mediterranean Port*, 1892. Watercolour 51.3 x 64.8 (20 ⅛ x 25 ½). Glasgow Museums: Art Gallery & Museum, Kelvingrove
105. George Henry, *A Galloway Landscape*, 1889. Oil on canvas 121.9 x 152.4 (48 x 60). Glasgow Museums: Art Gallery & Museum, Kelvingrove
106. George Henry and E. A. Hornel, *The Druids: Bringing in the Mistletoe*, 1890. Oil on canvas 152.4 x 152.4 (60 x 60). Glasgow Museums: Art Gallery & Museum, Kelvingrove. Reproduced by kind permission of The National Trust for Scotland
107. E. A. Hornel, *Kite Flying, Japan*, 1894. Oil on canvas 76.2 x 48.5 (30 x 19). NGS. Reproduced by kind permission of The National Trust for Scotland
108. Margaret Macdonald, Frances Macdonald and Herbert MacNair, *Poster for the Glasgow Institute of the Fine Arts*, *c.* 1896. Colour lithograph 236 x 102 (93 x 40 ⅛). Glasgow Museums: Art Gallery & Museum, Kelvingrove
109. Charles Rennie Mackintosh, *The Harvest Moon*, 1892. Pencil and watercolour 35.2 x 27.6 (13 ⅞ x 10 ⅞). Glasgow School of Art Collection
110. Margaret Macdonald Mackintosh, *The Opera of the Sea*, *c.* 1916. Oil and tempera with papier collé (after the now lost gesso original) 144 x 160 (56 ⅝ x 62 ½). Hessisches Landesmuseum, Darmstadt
111. Charles Rennie Mackintosh, *Revolving Bookcase for Hous'hill, Nitshill, Glasgow*, 1904. SNGMA
112. Jessie M. King, *I Pray You Hear my Song of a Nest* from *Seven Happy Days*, Christmas supplement to *The Studio*, 1913. © Dumfries and Galloway Council/National Trust for Scotland. Photo: The Mitchell Library, Glasgow
113. James Craig Annan, *Anna Muthesius*, *c.* 1900. Photogravure. SNPG. Reproduced by permission of T. & R. Annan and Sons, Glasgow
114. Sir Muirhead Bone, *A Shipyard Scene from a Big Crane*, 1917. Lithograph 46 x 35.5 (18 ¼ x 14). © The Hunterian Art Gallery, University of Glasgow
115. William Strang, *Grotesque*, 1897. Etching 20.3 x 17.8 (8 x 7). Glasgow Museums: Art Gallery & Museum, Kelvingrove
116. James Pryde, *Lumber: A Silhouette*, 1921. Oil on canvas 182.9 x 152.4 (72 x 60). SNGMA
117. Phoebe Anna Traquair, *Despair*, from the series of four embroidered panels *The Progress of a Soul*, 1899–1902. Silk and gold thread embroidered on linen 184.7 x 74.9 (72 ¾ x 29 ½). NGS
118. John Duncan, *Tristan and Iseult*, 1912. Tempera on canvas 76.6 x 76.6 (30 ⅛ x 30 ⅛). City Art Centre, Edinburgh © Estate of John Duncan 2000. All rights reserved DACS
119. George Dutch Davidson, *Envy*, 1898. Watercolour on paper 76.2 x 24.1 (30 x 9 ½). Dundee Arts and Heritage, McManus Galleries
120. Robert Burns, *Natura Naturans*, 1891, from Patrick Geddes' *Evergreen: The Book of Spring*, 1895. Photo Mitchell Library, Glasgow
121. Samuel John Peploe, *The Black Bottle*, *c.* 1905. Oil on canvas 50.8 x 61 (20 x 24). SNGMA. Reproduced with the kind permission of the artist's estate
122. John Duncan Fergusson, *The Blue Hat, Closerie des Lilas*, 1909. Oil on canvas 76.2 x 76.2 (30 x 30). City Art Centre, Edinburgh. © The Fergusson Gallery, Perth and Kinross Council
123. John Duncan Fergusson, *Les Eus*, *c.* 1910–13. Oil on canvas 213 x 274 (83 ⅞ x 107 ⅞). Photo © The Hunterian Art Gallery, University of Glasgow. © The Fergusson Gallery, Perth and Kinross Council
124. Francis Campbell Boileau Cadell, *Still Life (The Grey Fan)*, *c.* 1920–25. Oil on canvas 66 x 49.3 (26 x 19.4). Scottish National Gallery of Modern Art © The artist's family, courtesy of the Portland Gallery, London
125. Stanley Cursiter, *Rain on Princes Street*, 1913. Oil on canvas 51.4 x 61 (20 ¼ x 24). Dundee Arts and Heritage, McManus Galleries. © Estate of Stanley Cursiter 2000. All rights reserved DACS
126. Samuel John Peploe, *Ben More from Iona*, 1925. Oil on canvas 63.5 x 76.5 (25 x 30 ⅛). © The Hunterian Art Gallery, University of Glasgow. Reproduced with the kind permission of the artist's estate
127. George Leslie Hunter, *Houseboats, Balloch*, *c.* 1924. Oil on canvas 45.7 x 55.9 (18 x 22). Glasgow Museums: Art Gallery & Museum, Kelvingrove
128. Eric McBeth Robertson, *Love's Invading*, 1919. Oil on canvas 170.2 x 137.1 (67 x 54). City Art Centre, Edinburgh
129. Cecile Walton, *Romance*, 1920. Oil on canvas 100.6 x 150.9 (39 ⅝ x 59 ⅜). SNPG
130. Dorothy Johnstone, *September Sunlight*, 1916. Oil on canvas 152.4 x 107.9 (60 x 42 ½). University of Edinburgh. Copyright permission by courtesy of Dr D. A. Sutherland and Lady J. E. Sutherland. Photo: Joe Rock
131. John Duncan Fergusson, *Eastre (Hymn to the Sun)*, 1924 (cast 1971). Brass 41.8 x 22 x 22.5 (16 ½ x 8 ⅝ x 8 ⅞). SNGMA. © The Fergusson Gallery, Perth and Kinross Council
132. Hew Lorimer in his studio with *Our Lady of the Isles*, 1954–56. Granite, height 800 (315), now standing in South Uist. Photo courtesy of The Hew Lorimer Trust
133. Douglas Strachan, *Cain*, *c.* 1927, detail of stained glass, Scottish National War Memorial, Edinburgh Castle. Photo: Joe Rock. Reproduced by permission of Mainstream Publishing, Edinburgh
134. James Cowie, *Self-portrait: The Blue Shirt*, 1945–50. Oil on canvas 53.6 x 57.8 (21 ⅛ x 22 ¾). Collection of the University of Edinburgh. Photo: Joe Rock. Reproduced by permission of the artist's estate and Mainstream Publishing
135. James McIntosh Patrick, *Traquair House*, 1938. Oil on canvas 35.5 x 45.5 (14 x 18). SNGMA
136. Edward Baird, *Unidentified Aircraft (over Montrose)*, 1942. Oil on canvas 71.1 x 91.4 (28 x 36). Glasgow Museums: Art Gallery & Museum, Kelvingrove
137. Ian Fleming, *Gethsemane*, 1931. Engraving 34 x 44.3 (13 ⅜ x 17 ½). SNGMA. Courtesy of the artist's estate
138. William Wilson, *North Highland Landscape*, 1934. Etching 35.6 x 38.8 (14 x 15 ¼). SNGMA
139. David Young Cameron, *Wilds of Assynt*, *c.* 1936. Oil on canvas 102.1 x 127.9 (40 ⅛ x 50 ⅜). Courtesy of Perth Museum and Art Gallery, Perth & Kinross Council, Scotland
140. Charles Rennie Mackintosh, *Mont Alba*, *c.* 1924–27. Watercolour 38.7 x 43.8 (15 ¼ x 17 ¼). SNGMA
141. William McCance, *Mediterranean Hill Town*, 1923. Oil on canvas 92.1 x 61 (36 ¼ x 24). Dundee Arts and Heritage, McManus Galleries. Courtesy of Margaret McCance
142. William Johnstone, *A Point in Time*, 1929–38. Oil on canvas 137.2 x 243.8 (54 x 96). SNGMA. Reproduced with kind permission of Miss Sarah Johnstone
143. William Crozier, *Edinburgh from Salisbury Crags*, *c.* 1927. Oil on canvas 71.1 x 91.5 (28 x 36). SNGMA
144. William Gillies, *Skye Hills from Near Morar*, *c.* 1931. Watercolour on paper 38 x 56 (15 x 22). SNGMA. Reproduced with permission of The Royal Scottish Academy, Edinburgh
145. William Johnstone, *Celebration of Earth, Air, Fire and Water*, 1974. Oil on canvas 137.2 x 242 (54 x 95 ¼). SNGMA. With kind permission of Miss Sarah Johnstone
146. Hugh Adam Crawford, *Theatre*, *c.* 1935. Oil on canvas 65 x 65 (25 ½ x 25 ½). University of Dundee Museum Collections
147. William Crosbie, *Heart Knife*, 1934. Oil on canvas 60.3 x 43 (23 ¾ x 17). SNGMA. Courtesy of the artist's family
148. Donald Bain, *Children of Llyr*, 1945. Oil on canvas 107 x 94 (42 ⅛ x 37). SNGMA
149. William Gillies, *Mauve Landscape*, *c.* 1956. Oil on canvas 61.5 x 74 (24 ¼ x 29 ⅛). Collection Royal Scottish Academy, Edinburgh

150. Anne Redpath, *The Indian Rug*, *c.* 1942. Oil on plywood 74 x 96.5 (29 ⅛ x 38). SNGMA. © Estate of Anne Redpath
151. Sir William MacTaggart, *Wigtown Coast*, 1968. Oil on canvas 86.2 x 111.5 (34 x 43 ⅞). SNGMA. Courtesy of the artist's family
152. Robert Colquhoun, *Figures in a Farmyard*, 1953. Oil on canvas 185.4 x 143.5 (73 x 56 ½). SNGMA. © The Bridgeman Art Library, London/New York
153. Joan Eardley, *Wave*, 1961. Oil on board 121.9 x 188 (48 x 74). SNGMA. © Estate of Joan Eardley
154. Wilhelmina Barns-Graham, *Rocks, St. Mary's, Scilly Isles*, 1953. Oil on board 102.9 x 114.3 (40 ½ x 45). City Art Centre, Edinburgh
155. William Gear, *Autumn Landscape, September, 1950*, 1950. Oil on canvas 182.2 x 127 (71 ¾ x 50). SNGMA
156. Alan Davie, *Jingling Space*, 1950. Oil on board 122 x 152.5 (48 x 60). SNGMA. Courtesy of the artist
157. Edouardo Paolozzi, *Icarus* (1st version), 1957. Bronze 134.6 x 72 x 32 (53 x 28 ⅜ x 12 ½). SNGMA. © Eduardo Paolozzi 2000. All rights reserved DACS
158. William Turnbull, *War Goddess*, 1956. Bronze 161.3 x 48.3 x 40.6 (63 ½ x 19 x 16). Dundee Arts and Heritage, McManus Galleries. © William Turnbull 2000. All rights reserved DACS
159. Ian Hamilton Finlay with John Andrew, *Elegiac Inscription Stone:* See *Poussin*, Hear *Lorrain*, 1975. Stone. Reproduced courtesy of the artist. Photo: David Paterson
160. John Bellany, *Allegory*, 1964 (triptych). Oil on hardboard 212.4 x 121.8 (83 ⅝ x 48), 213.3 x 160 (84 x 63), 212.5 x 121.8 (83 ⅝ x 48). SNGMA
161. Elizabeth Ogilvie, *Sea Sanctuary*, 1989. Acrylic, ink, graphite, crayon and photograph on hand-made paper 244 x 366 (96 x 144). Photo courtesy of the artist
162. Calum Colvin, *Narcissus*, 1987. Cibachrome print 101 x 76 (39 ¾ x 29 ⅞). SNGMA. Photo courtesy of the artist
163. Will Maclean, *Land Raid Memorial*, 1996. Stone and earthwork, stone structure 281 x 500 x 150 (110 ⅝ x 196 ⅞ x 59). Sited at Gress, Isle of Lewis. Builder: Jim Crawford. Courtesy of the artist. Photo: The Stornoway Gazette
164 Maud Sulter, *Clio*, 1989. Colour photograph 120 x 95 (47 ¼ x 37 ⅜). Dundee Arts and Heritage, McManus Galleries
165 George Wyllie, *The Burning of the Straw Locomotive, 10.30pm, 22nd June, 1987.* Photo courtesy of the artist
166 George Wyllie, *The Straw Locomotive, 23rd June, 1987* (with its internal question mark exposed). Photo courtesy of the artist
167 David Mach, *Big Heids*, 1999 (detail). Welded steel, freight containers, each measuring 609.6 x 243.8 x 243.8 (20 x 8 x 8), total height *c.* 1000 (393 ¾). Reproduced by permission of North Lanark Council and the artist. Photo: David Peace
168. Kate Whiteford, *Calton Hill Drawings*, 1987. Crushed Skye marble laid in cut turf *c.* 60 x 160 (*c.* 197 ft x 525 ft). Photo Patricia & Angus Macdonald
169. Christine Borland, *Phantom Twins*, 1997. Hand-sewn leather, plastic replica fetal skulls, sawdust. Dimensions variable. Courtesy of the Lisson Gallery
170. Alan Johnston, *Installation shot*, exhibition in Haus Wittgenstein, Vienna. Canvas, charcoal, zinc white. Dimensions variable. Photo courtesy of the artist
171. Calum Innes, *Untitled: Exposed Painting Cadmium Orange*, 1995. Oil on canvas 110 x 100 (43 ¼ x 39 ⅜).Courtesy of Harry Handelsman & the Frith Street Gallery, London
172. Jack Knox, *Aftermath*, *c.* 1961. Oil on hardboard 104.1 x 129.6 (41 x 51). SNGMA. Courtesy of the artist's estate
173. Steven Campbell, *Painting in Defence of the Migrants*, 1993. Oil on canvas 272 x 256.5 (107 x 101). Glasgow Museums: Gallery of Modern Art. Courtesy of the artist
174. Alexander Moffat, *Poets' Pub*, 1980. Oil on canvas 183 x 244 (72 x 96). SNGMA. © the artist
175. Adrian Wiszniewski, *The Master Gardener*, 1988. Oil on canvas 183 x 183 (72 x 72). Private Collection, Australia. © Adrian Wiszniewski
176. Alexander Stoddart, *Hume*, 1997. Bronze 1 ½ times life size. Commissioned by the Saltire Society. Photo courtesy of the artist
177. Stephen Conroy, *Sir Steven Runciman*, 1990. Oil on canvas 122 x 76.2 (48 x 30). SNPG. Courtesy Marlborough Fine Art, London, Ltd
178. Alasdair Gray, *Jim Kelman* from *Lean Tales* by James Kelman, Alasdair Gray and Agnes Owens, Jonathan Cape, 1985. Courtesy of the artist
179. Ken Currie, *Great Reform Agitation: Unity is Strength*, 1987. Panel three of People's Palace History Paintings. Oil on canvas 218.4 x 251.5 (86 x 99). Glasgow Museums: The People's Palace
180. Jake Harvey, *Hugh MacDiarmid Memorial*, Langholm, 1982. Cor-ten steel and bronze 330 x 420 x 82 (130 x 165 ⅜ x 32 ¼). Dumfries and Galloway District Council. Photo courtesy of Runrig
181. Jake Harvey, *Cup Stones*, 1993. Kilkenny limestone 20 x 58 x 58 (7 ⅞ x 22 ⅞ x 22 ⅞). Private Collection, London. Photo: Jake Harvey
182. Gwen Hardie, *Fist*, 1986. Oil on canvas 158 x 220.5 (62 ¼ x 86 ¾). SNGMA. © the artist

Index

Figures in *italic* refer to illustration numbers.